CITIZEN FIRST, DESIGNER SECOND

Written by Rejane Dal Bello
Revised by Jayshree Viswanathan

Published by Counter-Print

This book is dedicated to
my loving parents Reinaldo
Dal Bello and Sueli Coutinho.

Contents

As someone who has spent more than 20 years working as a graphic designer, it goes without saying that I care deeply about design. It speaks to me like a language, which can't easily be understood by those who have not practiced and become fluent in it after making it their life's work.

But design is really something that touches and affects us all. We trust our eyes to help us make sense of the world; our earliest learnings come from what we can see. By improving our visual ability as we grow, what we are really improving is our ability to understand.

This is where visual language comes in. Our capacity to 'read' images means we can discover new perspectives beyond our own. And in an increasingly image-led world of brand and visual culture, images have come to shape our desires, our opinions, and our feelings.

We look at images every day. So as designers, we are not just in the business of creating pretty pictures. We are expanding people's abilities to see the world in new ways, beyond what is simply in front of their eyes.

Good design can make or break a brand, of course. But it can also give meaning and presence to causes and organisations that would otherwise never be seen or noticed. It is the difference between securing vital funding or being able to bring a message to a community. And it is the distinction between having a business purpose and having others come to value that purpose as much as you do.

As a designer, visual language gives me the tools to make something visible, worthy of time, attention and engagement. We all deserve to be able to tell our stories in a way that is reflective of our experiences and values. And it is both satisfying and humbling to contribute to a craft that lets me connect to society in this way. This is ultimately why what I do means so much to me. Design matters, because we all matter.

Rejane Dal Bello

DOII
ANY

IG IT
WAY

Doing it Anyway

If there is one thing that my design career has taught me, it's that you can never know what's in store. Even now, I still don't take anything for granted: there is so much to be learned and discovered through the process. I have come to terms with the fact that I have to create anyway – even if I don't know what will happen in future.

This makes a lot of sense when you consider how I came to design in the first place. Or perhaps, how it came to me.

My entry into the world of creativity was completely accidental. My family is a family of doctors, so my discovery of design and art as a teenager meant that I had to make a conscious stand against their expectations from a very young age. It wasn't easy. But the encounter I had with design and art was so deep and instant that I knew that I would never be able to give it up, even to please my parents.

I was born in Brazil, at a time when graphic design was not a career that was recognised or even known about by many people – so understandably my unconventional choice gave my parents a lot of anxiety. My father found my decision especially hard, but when a revelation shows itself as clearly as it did to me, there is no turning back.

I've come to understand that my parents don't understand visual language: it is foreign to them. And in a way, it is. Like a foreign language, it seems easy enough to learn from the outside – but in truth, it takes continued work and time to master it.

Until my moment of discovery,

the only exposure to graphic design that I had experienced was a book of anatomy, containing amazing illustrations that I loved to copy. Then at 15 years old, I went on an exchange trip to Lynchburg, in the US state of Virginia. Unlike at home, my American school timetable was the same every day. One of my chosen classes was art, and so I got the opportunity to practice it daily.

My drawing skills improved hugely, and I could feel that it made me truly joyful in a way nothing else had. At the end of the year, out of all the students, my painting was awarded 'Best in Show': something I just couldn't believe was true. Even though my anatomy drawings had shown I had creative potential, my parents had never recognised it – so I had not consciously recognised it in myself either. I simply drew because I loved it. But this event was a turning point, because it showed me for the first time that I could draw because I was good at it too.

That single moment gave me the validation and confidence I have relied on ever since, in order to live a creative life.

I returned home to Brazil with a new consciousness. After asking to see the drawings I did while on exchange, a friend I knew from jazz class told me that I should do graphic design. And I remember asking her, 'what is graphic design?' At that point, I still had not understood that being creative was something people did for work!

She tipped me off about a course that two other graphic designers were running, and so I chose to enrol on it. I knew from the very first class that

I'd found what I'd be doing with my life. For my final project I created an entire visual identity for a Mexican restaurant and that was that – I knew this was what I was meant to do. And I've continued on this path ever since.

Though my career is drastically different to what my parents had imagined for me, their teachings and presence as doctors have never left me. I've never forgotten that there is a human side to business, or that we should do what we can to help someone else. I believe this is the most valid way to spend one's life. This approach has given me both pain and joy over the years, but I don't know how to do things any differently.

I reason that if we really love something, there will be bumps along the way; it's never a continuously smooth ride all the time. And so

I have found it with my work. As design professionals, we always want the best outcomes, sometimes even more so than the person we are working for, because we recognise the value in visual language more than those who have not practiced and become fluent in it like us.

Since discovering design, I have had the most wonderful experiences. If I wanted to pursue money, or become the creative director of a design company, I could have done that. But I've chosen to let my career grow organically, without pursuing a set path or chasing conventional titles.

Maybe that makes me naive. But choosing to grow along with my experiences has been really important to me. I know that I have made sacrifices for my own growth and I am always surprised and proud of myself when I look back at everything I've achieved – I couldn't have done it any other way. It's not been easy to go through life making these seemingly counter-intuitive choices, especially when there are bills to pay and it is not easy to get by. But I have now come to the understanding that learning to successfully run my own business is ironically a skill that I need, if I am going to be able to keep living a creative life.

I call myself a graphic designer now, but I was also once a digital designer who knew how to program from scratch – although that seems like a distant reality now. I was even an artist at one point: I held exhibitions in New York and Seoul, and my artwork is still part of a Seoul museum. I've lived in four different countries and worked in some of the biggest branding studios in the world before starting my own studio, Studio Rejane Dal Bello. That led me to illustrate and create books, give lectures around the world, and now apparently I'm an author. After all this time and all these unplanned turns, I realise I have to just 'do it anyway', and see where it takes me next.

"I've never forgotten that there is a human side to business, or that we should do what we can to help someone else. I believe it is a perfectly valid way to spend one's life."

EARTH ART

A series of art works created by assembling images from Google Earth. The source material has been energetically re-arranged, re-worked and illustrated. The re-mixed results have been turned inside out, transforming their meaning in the process.

The series captures a new perspective, presenting images of infinity, fashioned by the imagination of the artist.

Collaboration for 3D creative animation with Aaron Baum.

Rejane Dal Bello

Doing it Anyway

Rejane Dal Bello

Doing it Anyway

Rejane Dal Bello

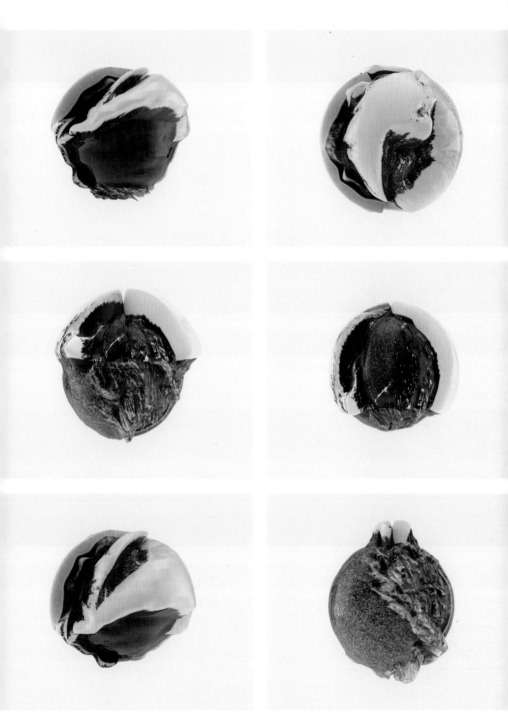

UPO 1 (UNIDENTIFIED PAPER OBJECT)

UPO is an occasional and bilingual printed matter published by Éditions Non Standard. UPO's aim is to emphasise a non-standard project from an 'undiscovered' artist. The 'Earth Art' project, from Rejane Dal Bello, was the emphasis for issue 1.

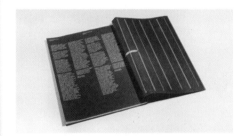

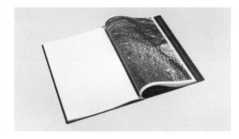

YOU DON'T

DON'T KNOW

You Don't Know

I had to understand the relationship between my work and technology quite early on in my career, just due to the simple fact that I graduated in the year 2000. At the time, 2000 was seen as 'the year', as it brought with it the dawn of a new millennium. We thought that by then the world would be super-technological and robotic, with flying cars above us and the Millennium Bug resetting all our computer systems.

In 1996, four years prior to the millennium, my art school teachers told us that there was no way we would succeed in a design career without learning everything about digital design. So like a good student, I did.

I learned everything there was to know about technology at the time, by hand – including CSS and HTML. At that time there were no YouTube tutorials as there are today. The only information came from fat 500-page textbooks, and there were no forums to find other people to ask questions about it either.

By the end of my art school years I was already employed at a web company, and juggling work and study. For my final art school exam, I showed off my tech skills by using Adobe Director – the multimedia program of choice at that time. I was as tech-savvy as a designer could possibly be at that time, so I felt totally ready for when the year 2000 came.

When the year finally arrived, to our surprise, there were no flying cars in the sky and the much-anticipated millennium bug did not really happen. In that moment, I understood that no amount of preparation could help me to really know what the future would truly look like.

If all the intellectual people in the world were predicting a future that did not come to pass, why was I limiting myself by doing what everyone else thought I should do, instead of doing what I really wanted to do? So I quit being a web designer and decided to focus on being a graphic designer instead.

Since then, whenever someone predicts that the future will be a certain way, I ask myself 'is this really likely'? The non-event of 2000 made me focus on the purpose of graphic design and its core values, and I have come to realise that the intelligence behind design, and the basic elements we work with, all remain the same.

It is only our tools and the ways

we choose to express our thinking that change over time. And with every new approach, each new generation of designers is able to fall in love with them all over again. None of us will ever know what is coming. We just need to follow our calling anyway.

"It is only our tools and the ways we choose to express our thinking that change over time. And with every new approach, each new generation of designers is able to fall in love with them all over again."

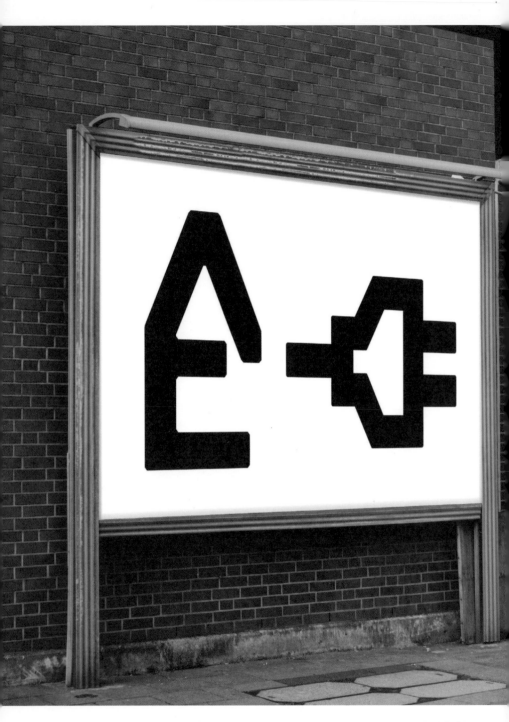

Rejane Dal Bello

LETIFY

Letify is an online platform that simplifies the lettings process for landlords - it allows them to customise the way they manage properties.

The design had to be as simple as the product - so Studio Rejane Dal Bello made the letter 'E' into a house. It created a brand device that allows Letify to stand out in all their communications and across any visual platform, simply by writing their name.

In collaboration with Chrys Naselos.

WE DON'T
CREATE
A BRAND

AD HAND, IT BECOMES.

We Don't Create a Brand. It Becomes.

I believe the idea that designers can 'make a brand' is ludicrous. It is impossible to know, at the time that we are working on the design of a brand, whether or not it will be successful.

Not even Milton Glaser, the master, knew while working on the identity for 'I heart NY' that it would be celebrated and loved by so many people. It was only intended to be a simple campaign that ran for two weeks – and yet it has become iconic and is still recognised today.
The assertion that success is within our control is not only untrue of a design, but also of any creative output: whether it is a TV show, movie, book... it is all unknown. What we can do, and maybe the only thing we can

do, is meet the brief in the best way possible. We can only identify the core purpose of any project, develop it in as honest a way as possible, and then leave it up to fate and pray.

Pray that it will resonate, pray it will become 'something'; pray that the thing you invested so much time into will prove useful to a group of people or to a service. Pray that all the forces out of our control come together and make sense of what we have created – because truly, 'making' a brand lies beyond the realm of design alone.

A good brand can actually have an awful brand identity. So where then, does our value as designers lie? Why does a brand need a good design, or a strong, unique identity? I do not believe in brand identity for its own sake. Rather, I believe that as designers we can use our skills to enhance a brand or product and make it valuable and relevant to its time.

A client once said to me that a good visual identity gives people confidence in your service. So, while a brand is not made solely by its design, we can help shape it into the best version of itself before chance and circumstance take over.

"The assertion that success is within our control is not only untrue of a design, but also of any creative output: whether it is a TV show, movie, book... it is all unknown. What we can do, and maybe the only thing we can do, is meet the brief in the best way possible."

Rejane Dal Bello

The needs of a city to flex, adapt and to constantly change – that's what fires this Dutch real estate developer's imagination and work.

This project was approached with that flexibility in mind and an identity was created that shows OVG as a modern, fluid and positive contributor to civic life.

Project developed while working at Studio Dumbar.

re/developers

Wilhelminakade 300 —— 3072 AR
P.O. Box 23413 —— 3001 KK Rotter
+31 10 290 87 77
info@avg.nl
www.avg.nl

Wilhelminakade 300 —— 3072 AR Rotterdam
P.O. Box 23413 —— 3001 KK Rotterdam —— The Netherlands
+31 10 290 87 77
info@avg.nl
www.avg.nl

Rejane Dal Bello

re/developers

OVG

KK Rotterdam —— The Netherlands

re/developers

OVG

P.O. Box 23413 —— 3001 KK Rotterdam —— The Netherlands

We Don't Create a Brand. It Becomes.

DESIGN CANNOT MAKE

REVOLUTION. ONLY PEOPLE CAN.

Design Cannot Make Revolution.
Only People Can.

I had the funny experience of being
'papped' at an anti-Brexit protest some
years ago, as part of which I had been
marching with a poster I had designed.

A few reporters chose to
photograph me, and I was surprised
to see myself splashed in several
newspapers the next day. It is not that
my sign was objectively 'better' than
any of the handwritten signs that other
protesters were holding, but it was an
unexpected reminder of our function as
designers. We have the ability to create
imagery that stands out, and in this
case even become newsworthy. We can
identify, clarify, highlight, simplify and
make it stand out. But we alone cannot
make revolution.

Rejane Dal Bello

As designers, our primary strength lies in distilling complex meanings into a simple, recognisable image – whether it's a corporate identity or a single visual form. Isn't that remarkable? It is an amazing skill to make things unique, help people to see differently, and give people or services visibility in an effective and considered way. But I don't think it can save the world per se.

Creatives are the in-between.

Design Cannot Make Revolution. Only People Can.

We are trusted to deliver messages, communicate ideas, organise thoughts and identify values... in this sense, we are able to help companies and individuals with skills and interests different to our own, move the world forward in the way they wish. Our power is always united with someone else's. But the contribution we bring is both necessary and powerful.

Design is a medium that works best in the service of something else or someone else. Our role is to champion someone else's work or idea. Society's needs are so diverse that we too are able to work, influence and collaborate in many forms and for so many different purposes. So what we do does matter – but I believe it matters most when we are in service to humanity.

This isn't to say that design is only of importance when it is used for 'important' subjects such as culture, politics or charity. Design can live in service to multiple causes – its application is as varied as society itself is. I think design is a big part of how society functions. So limiting the use of design to only 'worthy' causes, neglects the many other services that are necessary for our world to keep functioning. Design is important to make all of our lives better.

A protest poster cannot change the world by itself, but it can make us see the world from a different perspective. And so, while design can be used as a tool for change, only as people can we collectively make change happen.

> "Design is a medium that works best in the service of something else or someone else. Our role is to champion someone else's work or idea."

I LOVEU

The project I LovEU was developed in partnership with Chrys Naselos and Antoine Sandoz for the manifestation against Brexit happening in 2017 in London before Article 50 was triggered.

Design Cannot Make Revolution. Only People Can.

Design is not only about
aesthetics, it also plays
a vital role in society.
The 2010 European Design
Festival took place amid
seismic political changes,
and the identity designed
addressed those issues.

Inspired by the visual
language of protest
movements and European
flags, the work created
made the audience part
of the discussion.

Project developed while
working at Studio Dumbar.

Rejane Dal Bello

Design Cannot Make Revolution. Only People Can.

Rejane Dal Bello

Design Cannot Make Revolution. Only People Can.

DESIGN IS RELIGIOUS' WITHOUT

WITHOUT THE RELIGION

Design is Religious, without the Religion

It is quite unfashionable in the art and design world to be religious. But I have always found this quite ironic, when you consider how much of our work functions in mysterious and intangible ways. Inspiration and creativity have always seemed to me to be both miraculous and divine in equal measure.

The creative process is a path of the unknown. It is like walking down a street, never knowing if there will be an end or a reward, but we do it anyway. Maybe the wish and the will is bigger than us. It is like a force inside that drives us with a certainty that we cannot ever put our finger on. What else can we call this but faith? I see it no differently than those who feel there must be a bigger source

Rejane Dal Bello

in life, in which you can trust to give your life a direction and a meaning.

I don't think there are professionals who are more in need of faith than creative people. We start a project, we set a budget, we guarantee our clients it will be a success; even though we do not know what the outcome will be when we start.

The beauty of our profession is that we project and bring to life something that does not exist yet. That is why it is hard for us to measure the quantity of our work and be valued. We have to have faith that we will have a great idea along the way; and we must rely on so-called 'divine inspiration' though we cannot even know how, when or even if the idea will manifest itself. Our experience counts for a lot of course, but in design we are expected to deal with the unknown on a near constant basis.

So the only recipe I have come to rely on is based on the advice of Paulo de Tarso, otherwise known as Saint Paul. He tells us to, 'love, work, wait and forgive', a motto which I try to live by more generally, as well as apply to my design process:

Love

It is important for me to love the work I do. When I love a project, it brings empathy and understanding. Love gives me the perspective needed to design with ease: I find that time flies, and I have the presence of mind to recognise that everything will happen and blossom at the correct moment.

Work

Work is a fundamental part of being a creative professional and requires discipline and consistency. Most of the time we are just trying something out; we constantly bet on new ideas and projects, though even our best efforts do not guarantee they will always be successful.

Wait

Seasoned creatives can work without the anxiety of needing immediate success. Maybe success will not come at all.
Or maybe only someone else, or another generation will be able to complete the ideas that started with you.

Forgive

Our profession requires constant collaboration with people. It is impossible to make work by relying only on ourselves; we need several other skills apart from our own if we are to bring ideas to life. If we are to work with others, we must first respect their ways of doing things and 'forgive' the inevitable differences that will arise during the design process.

This project was a visual
identity to celebrate the
50th anniversary of the city
of Brasilia.

Studio Rejane Dal Bello
was inspired by Palácio do
Congresso Nacional, one of
the most iconic buildings
in the city. They took the
lines, shapes and forms of
the building and abstracted
them into blocks, which were
used to create the number 50.

Brasília 50 anos

O poeta Ezra Pound, ao se referir a Brasília disse "Make it new!".
E é justamente a combinação entre essa utopia – traço fundamental
de seu projeto, marca tão profunda que não desapareceu nesses
cinqüenta anos.

Brasília 50 anos

O poeta Ezra Pound, ao se referir a Brasília disse "Make it new!" .
E é justamente a combinação entre essa utopia – traço fundamental
de seu projeto, marca tão profunda que não desapareceu nesses
cinqüenta anos.

Brasília 50 anos

Rejane Dal Bello

Design is Religious, without the Religion

Rejane Dal Bello

DIGITAL PORN. IS FO

IS FOR
PRINT
R SEX.

Digital is for Porn. Print is for Sex.

Digital design is widely available, it's modern, sexy and you get off quite fast if you know what you're doing! Contrast this with print design, which you can touch and grab, and have a long-term relationship with if you treat it right. There is a feeling that has been around for a while, which is that digital will soon overtake print – but so far that hasn't happened, and I don't think it will.

We tend to be extremist when we have a new medium in town... but I don't approach life like this. We don't need to always substitute old things and replace them with new. Both mediums have their place and purpose – we just need to make the most of their respective strengths instead of always going for the latest thing.

Rejane Dal Bello

I remember the last time I developed a visual identity where the focus was still on print. It was for 'Alzheimer's Netherland' in Holland, whose main target group was naturally the elderly. Because they weren't generally as tech-savvy, everything was on posters and leaflets, and we printed them all from scratch.

There is still plenty of content that needs and deserves the attention of a good print design, that people will interact with in the physical world and will make us feel surprised when encountered on the streets or placed in our hands. There is also a lot of content that does not need to have a print element attached to it, or even need ink at all. I particularly love the animated posters we get nowadays, and they live exclusively on screens.

For me, this suggests that the

Digital is for Porn. Print is for Sex.

value of print is still as alive as it was before, it's just that we now have other ways of interacting with content too. And the two don't need to fight with each other, they can easily exist side by side.

So long live print, so long live digital and the new future mediums we will get to invent further down the line.

"The value of print is still as alive as it was before, it's just that we now have other ways of interacting with content too. And the two don't need to fight with each other, they can easily exist side by side."

alzheimer
nederland
alzheimer
nederland
alzheimer
nederland
alzheimer
nederland

oi.mer

eimer

eimer

Digital is for Porn. Print is for Sex.

ALZHEIMER FOUNDATION

The advance of Alzheimers and other forms of dementia is one of the greatest challenges the world is facing. The Alzheimer Nederland Foundation plays a vital role in raising awareness and funds for research in this field.

The disease causes significant memory loss – so the design work carried out explores the physical and emotional impact of Alzheimers, creating a distinctive visual identity that was used across all the Foundation's communication.

Project developed while working at Studio Dumbar.

Rejane Dal Bello

83

Rejane Dal Bello

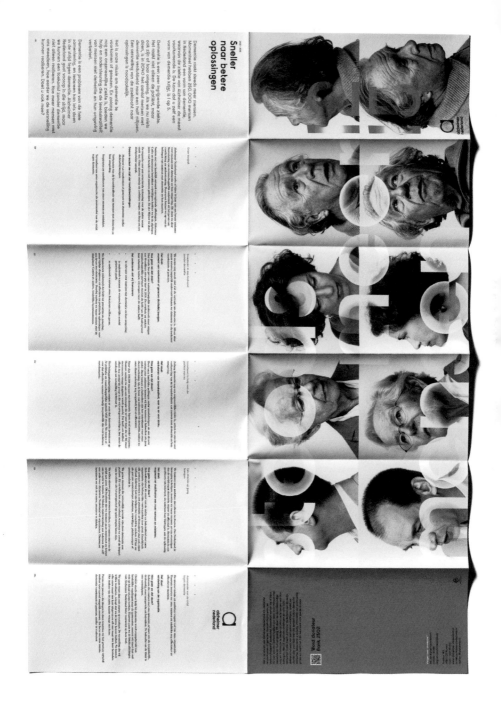

Rejane Dal Bello

I DON'T
LO
I FUCK T

VE TYPE.
PE.

I Don't Love Type. I Fuck Type.

Who said type needs to be legible? Perfect? Predictable? To a designer, perfection is not the point. The point is to do the job. Legibility is dependent on the goal. The only thing we know when we start a job is that it should be meaningful to the job. To be able to do that, we need to focus on doing the right thing, instead of doing the nice thing.

A design does not need to be perfect, but it must be right for the job in front of you. The idea that we have to be perfect is a misleading feeling, since it can block our creativity and cloud the understanding that life is always passing though us. Instead of discarding ideas right away, we should try to give them a go. This may push us towards a better idea which, even if it

Rejane Dal Bello

ends up being too wild for the client, it is always possible to tone down somehow. Doing it the other way around is much harder. If we play it safe with our creative process, we have no room to grow and no excess to refine from; it will already be pared back and probably highly predictable.

Nothing is static and what was perfect today will be different tomorrow. I have been in this business for more than 20 years now and a huge part of my portfolio is already dated. Was it perfect for that time? Maybe... but is it not perfect now? Maybe not... but it also might be again in the future.

Do what is right for the job at that time in place. We cannot predict the future and what will last. Do justice to your work at the time you do it, with the best skills you have, for the job at that moment in time. As for the rest, only time can tell.

This Brazilian non-profit organisation sees education as a vital
part of social transformation. They provide a diverse range of free
educational programmes, for all kinds of people. It's the most
important cultural and education institution in Sao Paulo.

Studio Rejane Dal Bello created an editorial system for printed
and digital material, to be used throughout the 12-month duration
of the courses – work that celebrated all forms of learning.

I Don't Love Type. I Fuck Type.

MÚSICA

6

● SUPERSÔNICA: MÚSICA ELETRÔNICA E EXPERIMENTAÇÕES SONORAS

SYNTH – 5 CAMADAS

Com Mau Schramm

Nesta atividade, serão ensinados os passos necessários para construção de um sintetizador de cinco camadas. Além das principais básicos da eletrônica, o público terá contato com as possibilidades do corte a laser para confecção do clarcaço do sintetizador.

Mau Schramm é pesquisadora, curadora, designer, produtora e desenvolve projetos sonoros e visuais.

Lab 2 (4° andar)
a partir de 16 anos • 15 vagas • 19/3 a 17/5 sextas (exceto 22/3 e 19/4)
• 19h às 21h30 • Grátis
Inscrições online pelo site sescsp.org.br/avendaquichela,
a partir de 27/2 (Credencial Plena) e 7/3 (público em geral)

7

ESTABILIZADOR DE CÂMERA

Com Coletivo Bodoque

O curso propõe uma introdução à bricolagem para soluções audiovisuais, apresentando as ferramentas, técnicas e práticas necessárias para a criação de equipamentos básicos para filmagem e fotografia. Esse módulo propõe a criação de um estabilizador tipo gimbal para câmeras, utilizando técnicas e ferramentas de marcenaria.

Formado por Chico Santos e Rafael Matlim, o **Coletivo Bodoque** atua na produção independente de conteúdo audiovisual e cultural, em diversos segmentos.

Lab 1 (4° andar)
a partir de 14 anos • 15 vagas • 26 a 28/3 terça às quinta
• 14h30 às 17h30

① R$ 25,00 ② R$ 12,55 ③ R$ 7,50

Inscrições online pelo site sescsp.org.br/avendaquichela,
a partir de 27/2 (Credencial Plena) e 7/3 (público em geral)

CRIANÇAS

37

● EU E O COSMOS

SELFIES COMO EXPRESSÃO ARTÍSTICA: OS QUATRO ELEMENTOS

Com Priscila Nemeth

Realização de exercícios criativos nos quais a prática da "selfie" servirá como ponto de partida para o desenvolvimento da percepção sensível, a partir dos quatro elementos: fogo, ar, terra e água.

Priscila Nemeth é fotógrafa e mediadora cultural, formada em Comunicação e Multimeios. Já atuou como arte-educadora em diversas exposições e ministrou oficinas sobre fotografia e literatura.

Lab 1 (4° andar)
a partir de 14 anos • 2 turmas, 1 por dia • 15 vagas por turma
• 9 e 10/3 sábado e domingo • 14h30 às 17h30
• Grátis • Entrega de ingressos 30 minutos antes, no local

20

● FESTA! FESTIVAL DE APRENDER

BORDADO TENANGO

Com Flávia Bombre

Curso inspirado na técnica tradicional de bordado tenango, originária do México. Serão abordados diversos aspectos dessa narrativa gráfica, uma cromática e significados estéticos. O grupo confeccionará um trabalho têxtil inspirado nos desenhos tradicionais mexicanos.

Flávia Bombre é ilustradora, artista têxtil, psicóloga e editora.

Lab 2 (4° andar)
a partir de 16 anos • 19 e 20/3 terça a sexta • 10h às 13h
• Grátis • Inscrições pelo site sescsp.org.br/festa a partir de 14/3, às 14h

21

I Don't Love Type. I Fuck Type.

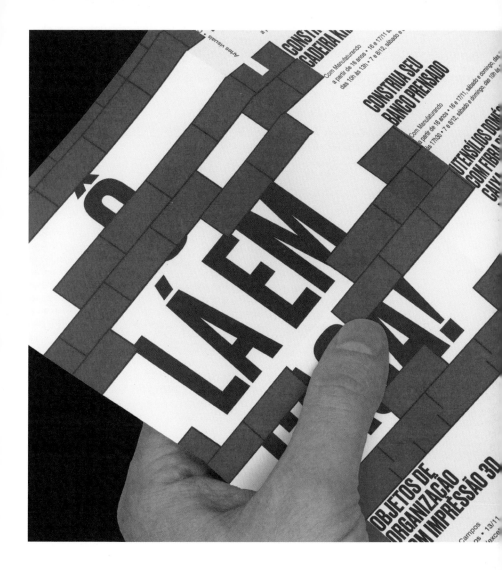

SESC CASA

This project celebrated the home – the courses, workshops, and other activities SESC devised for creating household objects. The design references the creative process of building things from scratch – the joy of making something that's uniquely yours.

I Don't Love Type. I Fuck Type.

Rejane Dal Bello

BE PLAYFUL

Playspace is an organisation that empowers employees to understand, challenge and change the rules that govern their lives and society.

The work was inspired by the idea of gamification – the joy of solving problems through play. A typographical set of shapes was created that playfully adapts to each framework.

Playspace

←

Rejane Dal Bello

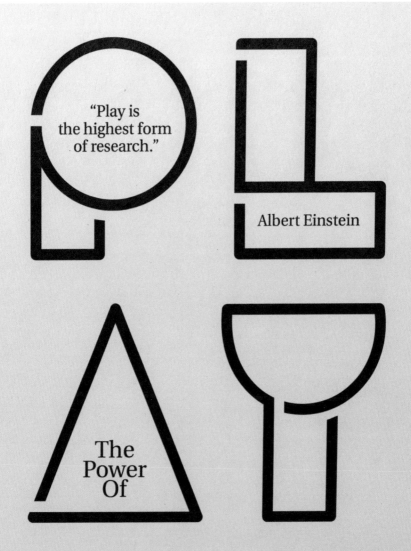

"Play is the highest form of research."

Albert Einstein

The Power Of

I Don't Love Type. I Fuck Type.

I Don't Love Type. I Fuck Type.

I Don't Love Type. I Fuck Type.

WE ALL HAVE A 'PAIR'

SHAWL OF SHAME'

We All Have a 'Drawer of Shame'

Every creative person has this drawer. In it are the projects that we are not proud of, or will never show in our portfolio. Maybe they did not turn out the way we wanted them to, or they were already too far from what we wished to do but they needed to be done anyway because of the money. We have all been there. Every time I put one more project in this drawer I always say to myself: it will be the last one. But I'm not really sure if it is avoidable.

When I see my biggest heroes out there shining in the world, I don't think there is much difference between my process and theirs (or at least that is what I imagine). Having recognition doesn't mean that their clients are more creatively satisfying to work with than some of mine. Of course, a client will be attracted by the quality of the designer they hire, but I believe that eventually the process turns out to be the same for us all. The moment we work for someone else we must contend with the other person's wishes and perspectives. This is hard enough to deal with in the first place, and it is made even more challenging because of the need to manage your creative vision and manage all the opinions which threaten the integrity or impact of your project.

I have done a few things through-out the years to keep my perspective and sanity. After being rejected for many jobs, losing pitches and seeing projects turn out differently to what I had hoped, I decided to collect my work in a sketch book form. For each project I work on, I now print thumbnails of the creative

process and I keep them inside a book.
I have around 20 books, and they have
become like a library of my work.
I learn from each book and they act as
a physical proof for myself that I have
been working hard and trying my best,
even if the final outcome is unlucky.

In a sense, these books have
become my therapist, they comfort
and reassure me. What also keeps me
sane is continuously creating projects
that are not related to clients at all;
and instead creating things whose only
purpose is to keep me going – which
I don't have to share with, or compromise
on for anyone.

In working this way, I have done
things that even turned out to be art
and I have participated in exhibitions
in two countries. In parallel, I have also
done projects in which I have had total
creative freedom, and kept teaching

Rejane Dal Bello

design – each of these have helped me to keep in contact with the creative field, in different ways.

Most recently I also have created my own self-initiated project, a book series about different childhood diseases called Dr Giraffe. The project is the culmination of five years of blood, sweat and literal tears. I'm the creator, the illustrator, the designer, the publisher and the investor. I financed the series with several corporate projects that paid well and gave me a financial payoff rather than a creative one. It is only thanks to them that I was able to fuel my creative life and continue to work on a personal project that I love and am passionate about. So though I call it my drawer of shame, maybe it is really nothing to feel ashamed of.

Collection of Rejane Dal
Bello's creative process
work within sketch books.

Rejane Dal Bello

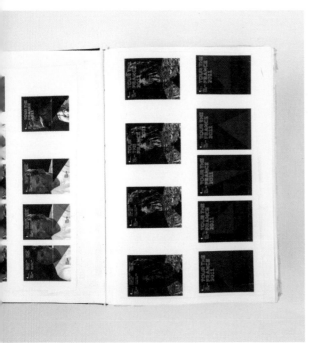

Rejane Dal Bello

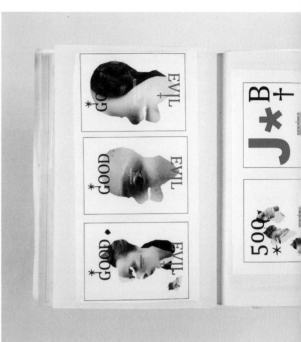

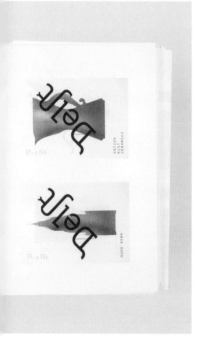

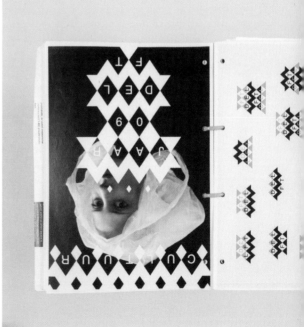

We All Have a 'Drawer of Shame'

WE CAN LI
WITH A BA
CAN'T LIV
WITH A TO

VE YEARS
O LOGO. WE
A MINUTE
OTHACHE.

We Can Live Years with a Bad Logo. We Can't Live a Minute with Toothache.

In 2019 there was a UK survey that said parents don't value the career prospects of creative subjects. Even with the increase in amazing and successful careers in the creative field, this suggests that the perceived value that creatives bring to the world is still very underappreciated.

Nothing has really changed from the time I started learning graphic design. I was born into a family of doctors, so this was my reality. My father is a doctor and my mother is a dentist; I have two older brothers and guess what... one became a doctor and the other a dentist. As a designer, the only thing I have in common with any of

Rejane Dal Bello

them career-wise is the letter D!
I understand that it can be a hard sell if
you come from a pragmatic perspective,
as they do. Because it is totally possible
for a person to carry on for years with
a bad logo... but they would not be able
to endure a single minute with a tooth
ache. In this particular context, design
has no role to play – but does that mean
it does not matter at all? Absolutely not.

Design matters and does have
a role to play in the world – but it is
often hard to grasp, as being creative
normally comes with an inherent
sense of inferiority that stops us from
understanding our value. The main
problem arises because we tend to
compare design with 'essential' services,
such as healthcare. But let's think here:
what else is essential? Of course, it is
not possible to live without the basics
of food, water, sleep and money. But

We Can Live Years with a Bad Logo.
We Can't Live a Minute with Toothache.

arguably emotion, which design and creativity affords us, is an essential too?

Our society is much more diverse than that, and in order to fulfil its many needs we need to have an array of tools and services at our disposal. Design is just one service for all these needs.

Good design has the ability to contribute and add meaning to our society. Of the many reasons why design matters, here are a few:

→ It is functional
→ It has meaning
→ It educates
→ It is playful
→ It adds emotional value
→ It solves problems
→ It sees differently
→ It has purpose
→ And most personally: design matters, because it matters to me.

Rejane Dal Bello

UPII

This charming visual identity was developed for a cupcake shop based in Brazil, feeding everyone from children at parties to wedding guests.

It's all about celebration. Love hearts, confetti, kisses… every element of this identity is designed to put you in a good mood.

We Can Live Years with a Bad Logo.
We Can't Live a Minute with Toothache.

www.upii.com.br

cu
p—cake

Rejane Dal Bello

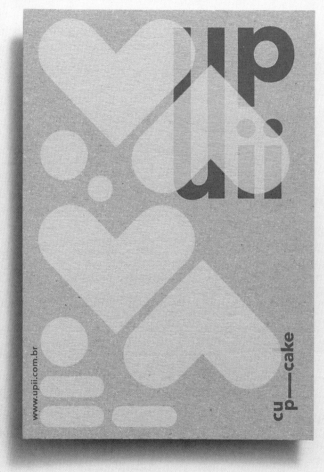

We Can Live Years with a Bad Logo.
We Can't Live a Minute with Toothache.

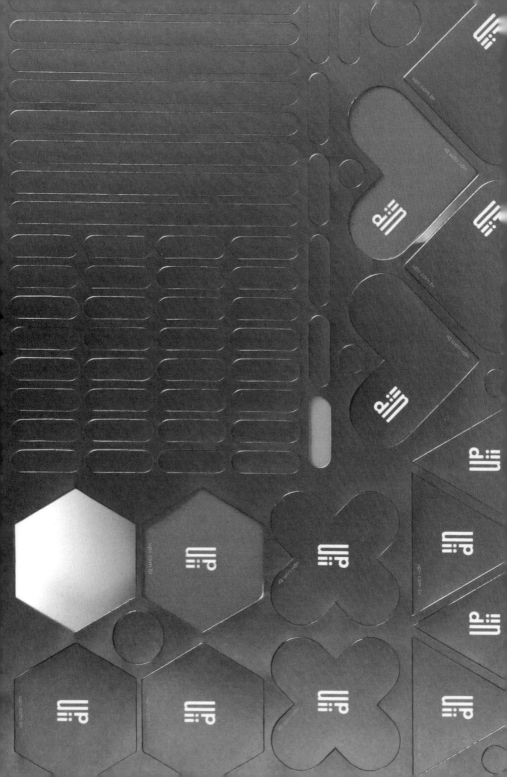

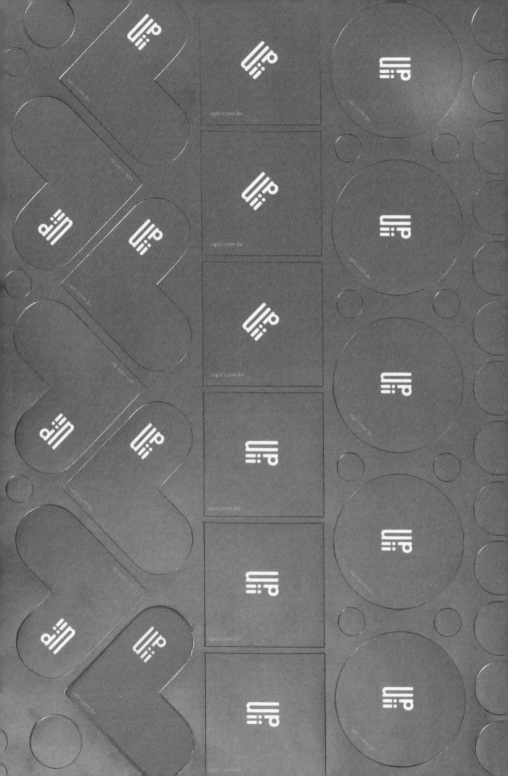

Rejane Dal Bello

FROM BEING B
BEING B

STUPID TO BEING PRAISED

From Being Stupid to Being Praised

I have been dyslexic my whole life. At six years old my parents took me to have a hearing test, after my teachers told them I could not follow basic letters and meanings. There were no known tests for dyslexia at this time, and nobody was even familiar with the term 'dyslexic'.

As a result, I struggled with school my whole childhood; I had to work much harder than the other kids and I had extra-curricular help for the next seven years to specifically help with my reading and writing. I almost flunked my literacy school year.

In hindsight, I am extremely thankful for not being weighed down with the label of dyslexia and perceived as someone with a 'disease' in my early

Rejane Dal Bello

years. But as with a lot of lessons in life, my dyslexia only made sense with time... and it has taught me to trust in the reasons why we are what we are.

It was only when I was 16 that things started to be put into perspective for me. I went to the USA, on an exchange program, and lived there for a year, during which time I enrolled in art class. At the end of the year I was given a huge surprise: out of all the students in the school, my work was chosen as the best in show – a recognition that literally changed my life. I had found that I could understand images far better than I had ever understood words, and that my unique understanding was something to be celebrated rather than stigmatised for. It was then that I decided I would pursue a creative life.

Since then I've found that by being dyslexic I am often able to jump straight to a fully formed idea or solution without knowing how. As a designer, my dyslexia has actually proved to be one of my biggest assets, helping me to distil complex meanings into a simple, iconic image – whether that's a corporate identity or a single image.

We never understand our so-called shortcomings in the moment, but there always comes a time where it all makes sense.

"As a designer, my dyslexia has actually proved to be one of my biggest assets, helping me to distil complex meanings into a simple iconic image – whether that's a corporate identity or a single image."

Rejane Dal Bello

From Being Stupid to Being Praised

Rejane Dal Bello

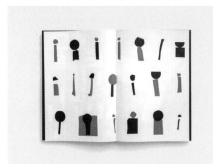
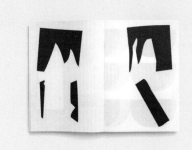

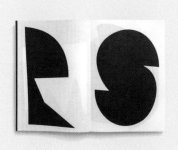

UPO 3
Studio Rejane Dal Bello created the identity for UPO and also designed
this third edition, which featured Marion Baitalle. This amazing
artist helps children to write their names in a non-traditional way,
so they feel there is no room to fail.

From Being Stupid to Being Praised

Rejane Dal Bello

RATI
TELLS.E
GUI

NALE
MOTION
DES.

Rationale Tells. Emotion Guides.

We respond to an image emotionally and not intellectually. The times I have reached into my gut and emotions are when I have been able to create my most honest work. Being in the creative field is one of the most sensitive and fragile jobs in the world, because we pour our very selves into it. We have to reach deep into our most vulnerable emotions to be able to create something that will be considered unique, from an honest place. In order to create something 'new', we need to see things, imagine impossibilities, and bring people along with us to the future we are creating.

If you are not in the creative field, and required to reveal your vulnerabilities in this way, it will be hard to understand this point of view. But it also removes

Rejane Dal Bello

the right to critique or judge what we do. If you haven't been exposed to what we do, you cannot know our perspective.

But if you are here, prepared to show up and, like me, be kicked down or disappointed many times... you already have my utter respect. We don't have to succeed, but in trying and trying again, I believe that success is eventually found.

In companies where strategy is too controlling and overly involved in the design process, I have found it really hard to be able to work from that honest place. In order to create, we first need to have our own space. If we are too confined already, it is hard to imagine more than what we can already see.

As Benjamin Disraeli said, 'life is too short to be small'. To live a small life is to live a life that is closed off and limited. In order to create I need to overflow, go beyond my comfort zone, and get together with others with whom I can communicate and share. My life may end up being short, but I hope it will never be small.

This is not the same as having fame or importance. A lot of people are famous but not important. 'Important' does not mean we need to find the cure for cancer, but that in the eyes of the people who surround us, we are there to support, help and receive help in return. Life is made up of these smaller parts – we should not expect that it is only the big gestures that will get us where we hope to be.

"To live a small life is to live a life that is closed off and limited. In order to create I need to overflow, go beyond my comfort zone, and get together with others with whom I can communicate and share."

Rejane Dal Bello

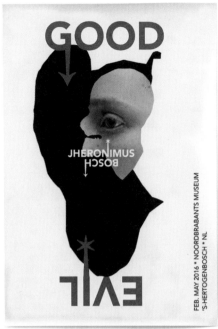

HIERONYMUS BOSCH - 500 YEARS
The Dutch city of Den Bosch
is a place synonymous
with the celebrated artist
Hieronymus Bosch. This
identity for the city
marked the 500th anniversary
of his death in 1516.

His work is known for its
deep insight into humanity's
desires and deepest fears
- the design reflects
the duality of his art
and his city in a series
of arresting images.

Project developed while
working at Studio Dumbar.

ALZHEIMER FOUNDATION
Visual identity for The Alzheimer Nederland Foundation, who raise
awareness and funds for research in this field.

Project developed while working at Studio Dumbar.

verlies

**alzheimer
nederland**

KOSTERIJLAND 3
POSTBUS 183
3980 CD BUNNUK

Elke derde dinsdag v/m
19.00 - 21.30 uur
www.alzeimer-nederland.nl

Rotterdam

Rejane Dal Bello

MAKING AN IMAGE

MEANS YOU EXIST

Making an Image Means You Exist

I have been working for one client
for over 15 years now. She opened
a children's hospital in Peru that offers
free services; and before the hospital
had even started to be built, she asked
me to design a logo and a visual identity
for it. She felt she needed that in order
to be able to give shape to her dream.

Though she did not yet have an
address, she had an image that meant
her dream was tangible and existed.
With this image in hand, she could
look for funding, prove her intentions
and communicate her ethos and the
vibe that she wanted to express as a
business. In other words, she could get
her partners to believe in her and trust
that she was for real.
Thoughtful branding work can do

Rejane Dal Bello

this. It is invaluable in giving you that solid ground to build upon. Only eight years after developing a logo and the identity for her was she able to officially open her hospital. Until that date, her brand identity was the sole representation of her entire vision.

In the 15 years since the hospital was first created, and in the five years since the hospital opened, there have been 4,760 lucky children who have received treatments, operations, therapies, and other medical services free of charge. Around 300 children are operated on each year, and 8,000 consultations are carried out free of charge. Not only are children from the local area benefited, but also children from all over Peru.

Her approach reminds me of musician Quincy Jones, who said about his upbringing, 'I wanted to be what

I see... I only saw gangsters out on the streets. So I wanted to be one'. People take what they see as the only true interpretation of their surroundings.

This is one of the reasons I believe in always pushing the client to make the best images, and deliver the best project – because we are influencing our environment and what people believe is possible. Images are not as naive as we think, and not so insignificant as we may want to believe. They are the manifestation of our dreams and hopes for what we wish to see in the world.

Buena Salud

Buen

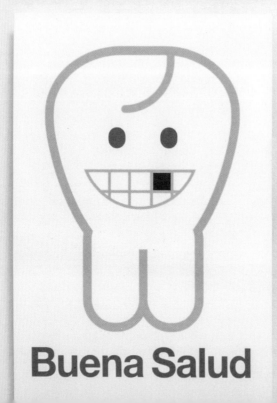

Buena Salud

Buena

Salud

Buena Salud

x-ray

Salud

Buena Salud

Libro para Colorear

PAZ HOLANDESA
Paz Holandesa is a free children's hospital in Arequipa, Peru.
It was founded in honour of child cancer patient Tony Rojas
Molleapaza, whose memory is cherished by the city.

The job was to create an identity that could delight, engage and
distract the children at the hospital - so Studio Rejane Dal Bello
created PAZ and friends - a series of warm, friendly characters
who could soften everything from signage to posters all over
the building.

Since 2005, PAZ and friends have gone from logos to stationery, folders,
cards, signage, wall paintings, games and editorial material.

Making an Image Means You Exist

Baño de Hombres

Baño de Mujeres

baño privado

doutora

doutor

inscription

niño

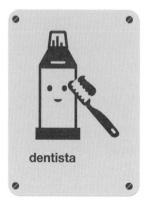

dentista

rampa para discapacitados

Rejane Dal Bello

Making an Image Means You Exist

Jaarverslag
2019

Rejane Dal Bello

Making an Image Means You Exist

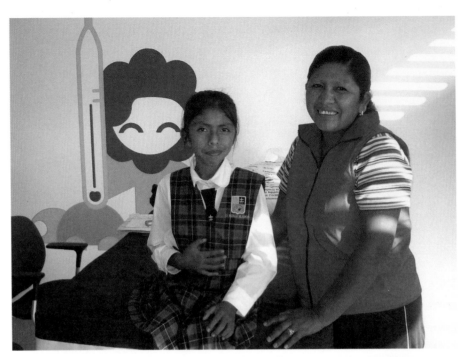

Rejane Dal Bello

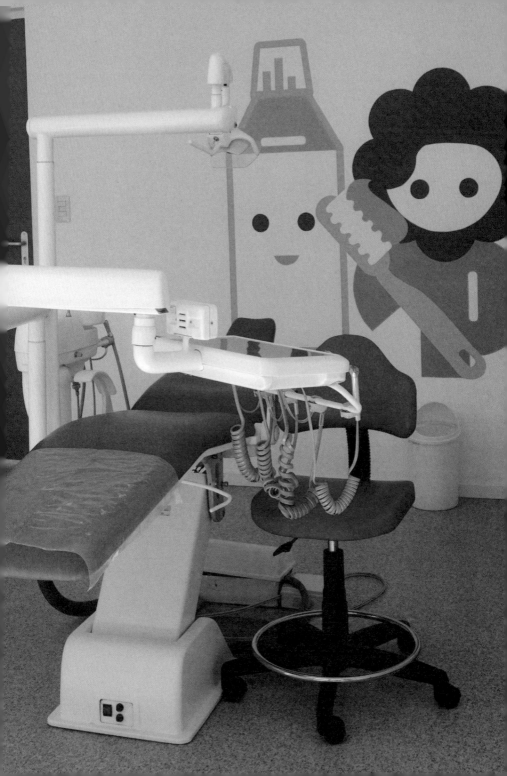

WHAT AN
WITH MY
TO HELP

I DOING
SKILLS
OTHERS?

What am I Doing With My Skills to Help Others?

I was 17 when I started art school, and I started to do social work at the same time. Because of these two commitments I started to see two completely different realities: one was a harsh reality shaped by poverty, with kids abused by families or living in really deplorable situations, while the other was all about imagination, positive colours, shapes and optimism about a future.

That for me was a conscious moment when I really started to think: what am I doing with my skills to help others?
That moment of self-consciousness actually changed the whole course of my life. After that I kept both worlds

alive. I went on to do a master's course, specialising in social design, where I worked on a project around preventing long-term homelessness and joined causes and met people who were also interested in the type of projects I wished to get more involved in. So alongside my bread and butter graphics work, pro bono projects will continue to be a huge part of how I see my role in the world of design. I believe I am a citizen before I am a designer, so it's hard for me not think on a bigger scale.

That's what keeps me going, because when I work with big clients it's hard at times to maintain a sense of artistic integrity. I always look for things that I feel I can learn from in a humanistic way, and retain creative freedom by doing. This is something which is extremely important for me to feel alive.

Everything is temporary. Being aware and conscious of the difficult sides of the world, of its suffering, I am able to learn from it and help causes or bring beauty into situations with my design. As designers we can create the world we want to see, we have the skills to extract the positive from any brief – and that is what makes me wake up every day and go to the studio.

Doing social work and coming from a lesser-developed country, I believe that occasionally working for free is essential to empower another person or cause. I think we should be able to help each other with our skills. This is the reason I use my design skills to support socially-led projects along the way, so that in some small way I can give projects that are important for society a bigger chance of success and survival.

Rejane Dal Bello

DR. GIRAFFE

Explaining an illness to a child, whether common or serious, is
no easy feat. It's something every parent must do, but knowing what
to say and how to say it, can be a huge challenge. Often, they simply
don't have the medical knowledge needed to explain a disease and
provide much-needed comfort.

This is where Dr. Giraffe comes in. With simple words and pictures,
and grounded in medical truth, each book in the series tells a story
about one childhood disease – ranging from common ailments to rare
conditions. To mum and dad's relief, Dr. Giraffe can do what they
perhaps cannot: help young patients make sense of what they are going
through, in a way that is clear, medically accurate, and (no less
importantly) pleasant to read.

Created, illustrated, designed and published by Rejane Dal Bello
Words and story by Jayshree Viswanathan
Medical strategy by Stefan Liute
Supported by Marjan van Mourik

What am I Doing with my Skills to Help Others?

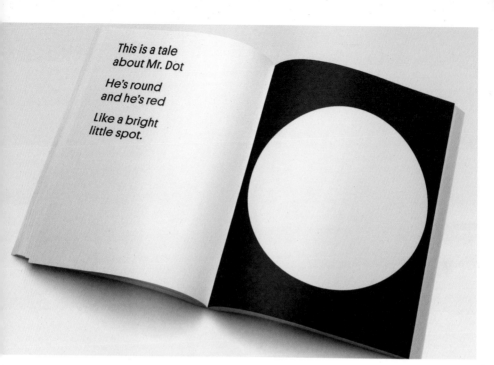

This is a tale
about Mr. Dot

He's round
and he's red

Like a bright
little spot.

itchy!

Rejane Dal Bello

What am I Doing with my Skills to Help Others?

Dr. Giraffe

land OF THE big
A little story about leukaemia

alf

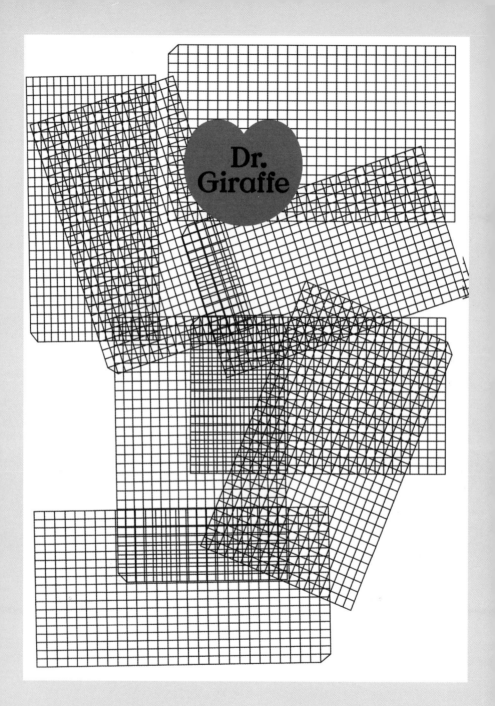

Dr.
Giraffe

Rejane Dal Bello

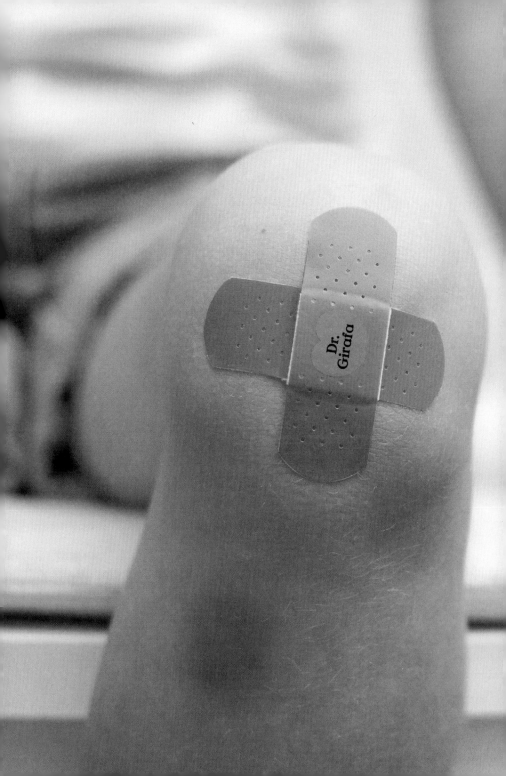

CITIZEN FIRST,

DESIGNER SECOND

Citizen First, Designer Second

Designers are always in service to something or someone else. Design isn't 'the thing', it is never the hero by itself. Design is a medium between things, and instead communicates what 'the thing' is. It informs 'the thing'. It identifies 'the thing'. We are in service to 'the thing'. So does this mean that design matters as much as the subject it is dealing with?

Designers tend to think they are the heroes of the projects, but I beg to differ. The projects that have been the most successful for me were the ones that ended up changing me, not the ones where I have changed my client.

With design I can learn about the world. The world's needs are so diverse, and I believe that design has the power

Rejane Dal Bello

to navigate through and contribute to them. So there is no work that is 'more important'. All work is important if it is serving a need in the world. The true value of any work is what it has done within you. How much has it changed you? How much have you changed by working with it?

We keep comparing works against one another. But the real work is the transformation we make within ourselves. If the work doesn't transform you intimately, you might receive a traditional merit for it but nothing more than that.

Ultimately it is not the job itself that offers value, but the value that it will give to you that is important – and this, I have found, can come from any job.

UPO 2
This issue is dedicated to
the work of the photographer
Xenia Naselou. She gives
us a glimpse of what is
happening on the island
of Lesvos in Greece. Observed
with a beautiful sensitivity,
without being intrusive to
those who've been through so
much due to the immigration
crisis, her work is a silent
documentation of the traces
it has left.

I wish I was there   J'aimerais être là
Xenia Naselou   Upo II

Élodie Boyer
Rejane Dal Bello
Frédéric Lambert
Jean Segui

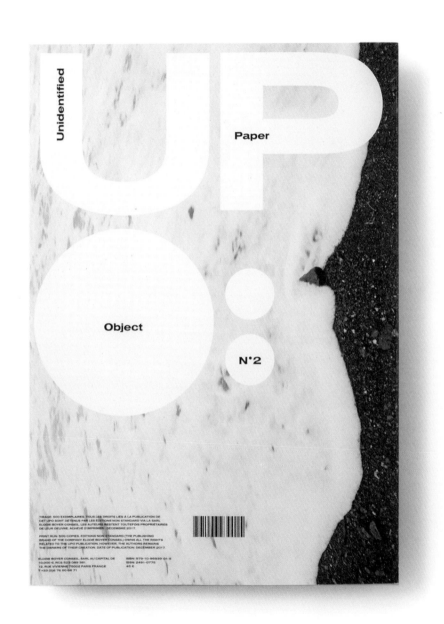

Citizen First, Designer Second

OTIS WORKSHOP WITH BLACK LIVES MATTER
This workshop was hosted by Rejane dal Bello and Chrysostomos Naselos
with Black Lives Matter creative director Noni Limar at Otis LA.
The brief was to select one of the 13 guiding principles BLM stand
for to design your campaign poster.

The aim was to:
→ Move away from the death narrative
→ Create something vibrant, joyful, bold and impactful
→ Embrace the black renaissance
→ Celebrate five years of Black Lives Matter.

Citizen First, Designer Second

SSH

SSH Utrecht is a social housing organisation for young people and students, mostly from the university and the various colleges in Utrecht. The main focus of the concept is 'individuality versus community' – meaning several students, with different backgrounds and characters, living together and sharing the same space.

Rejane Dal Bello

Project designed while at Studio Dumbar.

Citizen First, Designer Second

WE WORK FOR THE CLIENT AND

FOR THE DESIGN COMMUNITY

We Work for the Client and for the Design Community

There are two laws of nature that para-doxically co-exist: the law of progress and the law of destruction. We know that in order for things to progress, something will have to be destroyed.

Any project we ever do, no matter how amazing or how long-lasting you think it is, will be cast aside eventually. Most of the jobs we do today have a lifespan of five to ten years, or until the strategy of the company changes, whichever comes first. When this happens, the visual identity of the company will inevitably change – and even if you are the one who did the initial work, you might not be the one who is chosen to continue it further.

This 'passing on' of a project for the next designer makes me aware

Rejane Dal Bello

that my responsibility is not only to the client, but to the design community at large. Knowing that any job we do will be worked on by another designer in a few years, we should do our very best to push the boundaries of the client at that moment in time.

We have to think that any job we do will be worked on by another designer at some point. So it pays to push the boundaries, not only for yourself, but for the next designer that might get the job after you.

If you have done your job to the fullest, where you tried to push the envelope and visually evolve the market to the maximum, using your best skills at the time... then the next designer, years later, can pick up where you left off and push your work even further. They might not even need to do as much pushing as someone did before you. Good designers work for the progress of the job itself but also the progress of the design community we are part of.

Therefore, we have to thank every single generation, and pay tribute to the design heroes that came before us and pushed the boundaries to allow us to push our design work further... and further and further, as each successive generation passes.

"If you have done your job to the fullest, where you tried to push the envelope and visually evolve the market to the maximum, using your best skills at the time... then the next designer, years later, can pick up where you left off and push your work even further."

Rejane Dal Bello

Rejane Dal Bello

OPEN LOOP
Open Loop is a New York bus sightseeing brand – working in one of
the noisiest, busiest, most visually demanding cities in the world.
Making Open Loop seen is a huge challenge.

But they have something other brands don't: a fleet of giant moving
billboards, where the product and the brand are one.

Visitors to New York want to feel totally immersed – so Rejane
Dal Bello created the most American-looking busses in the world.
They stand out, even in the heaviest traffic.

In collaboration with strategist Elodie Boyer and designer
Danny Kreeft.

DON'T EXPECT THE PERFECT

GARDEN TO BE ABLE TO FLOURISH

Don't Expect the Perfect Garden to be Able to Flourish

It has been more than 20 years since I began working professionally as a graphic designer, and the only thing I can confirm that I have learned in this is: we don't have as much control as we like to think over our lives or careers.

Because of this realisation, I started collecting my work in sketch book form to learn from it and remind myself that the path is diverse, and that we have no idea when our efforts will take root and flourish and when they will not. Despite my best efforts sometimes, a project does not make it through the final stage or it is not picked up and fails. It is heart-breaking every time. But in spite of the odds, I have learned this as well: don't expect the

Rejane Dal Bello

perfect garden to be able to flourish... we should still flourish nonetheless!

We cannot really control the circumstances around us, but one thing remains in our hands: the power to be the best we can be, in any circumstances that are put in front of us. The potential to flourish is always there. And when a project is accepted and does go the way we wanted to go... it is fucking amazing!

I don't expect perfection. The creative path is full of uncertainty, but the point is to learn something from the journey each time. What comforts me is that you might be feeling the same way while reading these words. We are all learning, with no exceptions.

The ones who can lead are the ones that have more experience in a field, not because they are better than you are. If you are currently leading, it's because you have acquired knowledge at something, but there will surely be other areas in which you too are following.

Being big, famous or important in this world counts for little. The ability of every flower is to flourish to its full potential where it was planted. If you have not flourished within small or little opportunities, you will not flourish much when you have big opportunities either. So, cultivate your skills where you find yourself in this current moment, instead of waiting for your garden to be perfect.

"The creative path is full of uncertainty, but the point is to learn something from the journey each time. What comforts me is that you might be feeling the same way while reading these words. We are all learning, with no exceptions."

Rejane Dal Bello

CREATIVE PROCESS – ALZHEIMER NEDERLAND FOUNDATION
Developmental sketch book work for The Alzheimer Nederland Foundation.

Images taken from the private sketchbooks of Rejane Dal Bello.
Project developed while working at Studio Dumbar.

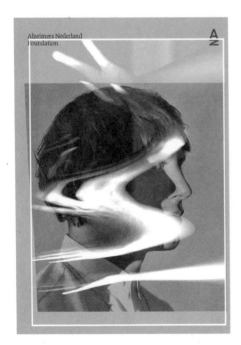

Rejane Dal Bello

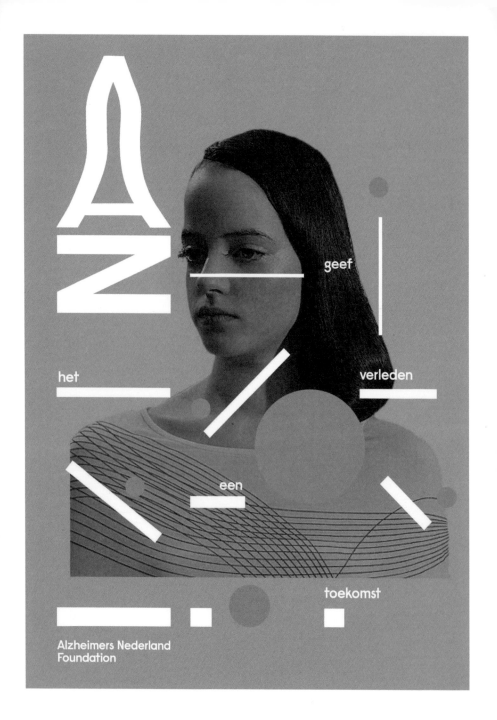

AZ
geef
het
verleden
een
toekomst

**Alzheimers Nederland
Foundation**

Alzeimers Nederland
Foundation

A
Z

don't
don't
forget

Don't Expect the Perfect Garden to be Able to Flourish

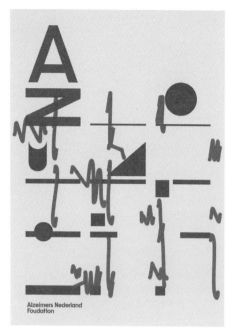

Alzeimers Nederland
Foudation

don't
forget
those
who
already
forgotten

Alzeimers Nederland
Foudation

geef

het het het

den
leden
verleden

een

toekomst

Alzeimers Nederland
Foundation

Iedereen
LAchen
gelijk-
huilen
waardig
en wijzer
worden

Alzheimers Nederland
Foundation

Rejane Dal Bello

Don't Expect the Perfect Garden to be Able to Flourish

Rejane Dal Bello

DESIGN
REVI

ALS
ITSELF

Design Reveals Itself

The creative process reveals itself through action. It is only by doing, that the answers come. It is in the act of living and breathing the idea daily, bit by bit, that we can strengthen the work we do.

Nobody gains recognition right at the start. Our greatest heroes were once unknown. They too were working, and one day life revealed them to us – but they were there all along, alive and getting on with their lives and their professions just like us.

They grew through the process of doing. From them we can learn that there is no recipe for success. It is only by having consistency of thought that we can keep pursuing the idea of life and work and become stronger as a result.

Rejane Dal Bello

Right after I moved to London, I went to give a lecture at the Bath School of Design. After the lecture, one of the teachers of the school commented that, 'I had run the marathon of design'. I was only 34 at the time, so I didn't really know what to think. It is definitely a compliment, as I can't even imagine running 26 miles in real life. It has also certainly been a hell of a run, starting as I did at 17 and working intensively in design since then. I did not start knowing it all.

The path is definitely diverse and surprising. I could never have thought this would have been my path in my wildest dreams... life reveals itself while we are experiencing it. I had some raw talent, but the rest was revealed and experienced as I have gone through life.

This project celebrated an international exchange between Dutch and Chinese colleges. The type is deliberately chosen to clash, so it represents the imperfections and unpredictability that makes collaboration interesting.

Dutch Design College is an initiative by Michel de Boer.

DUTCH DESIGN COLLEGE
P O W E R E D   B Y: Willem de Kooning Academy

DDC

DUTCH DESIGN COLLEGE

POWERED BY: Willem De Koning

OPEN DAY
DDC

SHANGHAI:
Street / Time by St. FRANKLIN 28,
20:00 hrs - 21:00

Rejane Dal Bello

LECTURES

DDC
DUNBAR DESIGN COLLEGE
POWERED BY Wilson le Kerning Academy

EXAMN
EXAMN

Rejane Dal Bello

WHER
IS LIFE
IS CH

THERE THERE ANGE

Where there is Life, there is Change

My path has been incredibly diverse.
Every phase has been a transformation.

I started as a web designer doing programming and processing, then I quit everything and became a graphic designer and teacher. I did a master's course and ended up becoming its teacher, worked in the biggest branding studios in Rio de Janeiro, Rotterdam and London, and studied under major teachers like Milton Glaser and Richard Wild in New York. Now I have my own design studio, which, in the process of running it all by myself, still leaves me feeling like a beginner from time to time.

Along the way I created a project that was picked up as 'art', exhibited in galleries in New York and Seoul and has

Rejane Dal Bello

since been acquired by a contemporary South Korean museum. Meanwhile, I have self-published three books, which I also came up with the concept for and illustrated, in four different languages. I have travelled the world giving lectures and teaching in art schools, and I'm now doing the one thing I thought I could never do: writing a book.

I have just tried my best to keep living... and in the process change has found me, and I hope will continue to do so.

Sequoias are some of the oldest living things on planet earth. There are some in California that are over 3,000 years old. They are literally giant trees, with trunks so wide it takes as many as 20 people to encircle them, and so tall that they rise more than 30 metres into the sky.

But the seed of a sequoia fits in the palm of a hand and takes years to start growing upwards. In the first four to five years, a sequoia seed spends most of its time literally growing down and taking root, for it is only by having strong roots that it can grow to such colossal size. This is also true of many other trees that have the potential to live for hundreds and thousands of years. It is all a process.

Now, you might say, 'wow... that's some process'. To that, I would reply, 'then plant cabbage'.

Cabbage is a delight! You plant it, and after only a month and a half it will have grown beautifully! All it needs is a good rain shower to grow. This too is a process, but with very different results.

In life we have to choose whether we want to be a sequoia or a cabbage.

Rejane Dal Bello

Having chosen design, I see every project as having the potential to be a sequoia. Even if the result does not immediately seem visible, we are slowly being transformed, in our own time.

When you are feeling lonely, remember this image and the goal that lies beyond the present moment will come back into your sights.

"Having chosen design, I see every project as having the potential to be a sequoia. Even if the result does not immediately seem visible, we are slowly being transformed, in our own time."

Tour poster promotion
for Australia's most
famous punk rock singer,
Courtney Barnett.

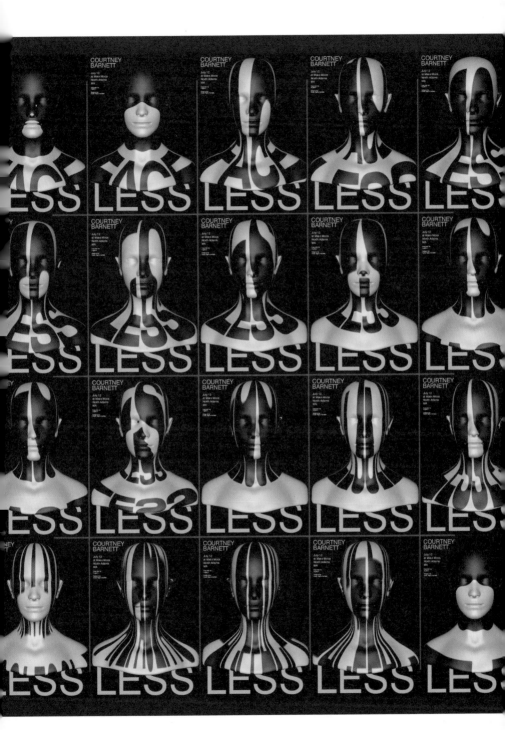

Where there is Life, there is Change

COURTNEY
BARNETT

July 12
at Mass Moca
North Adams
MA

Supported by:
Vagabon

Designed by:
Studio Rejane Dal Bello

LESS

THE PARIS INCIDENT never AGAIN Paul

Rejane Dal Bello

juste pour vous Juliette

Where there is Life, there is Change

NO MORE TEAR-JERKING WC LITS AMELIE

Rejane Dal Bello

ORANGE POSTERS
Orange developed this initiative to respond to customers, assuring them that bad incidents they experienced in the past would never happen again.

Rejane Dal Bello helped develop a personal approach, with each poster seemingly being created for each customer, echoing Orange's unique promises.

Project developed while working at Wolff Olins.

Rejane Dal Bello

Where there is Life, there is Change

FALLING LOVE
'Falling Love' is an animation developed for the Demo Motion
Festival in Amsterdam.

THE TYPOGRAPHIC CIRCLE
Poster designed by Rejane Dal Bello for her lecture
at The Typographic Circle.

Rejane Dal Bello

typo

f**k typo
Studio Rejane Dal Bello
Thursday 21st February 2019

St Bride Library
14 Bride Lane
London EC4Y 8AU

typocircle.com
info@typocircle.com
@typocircle

SIMPLY LIKING CREATIVITY

ISN'T LIVING CREATIVELY

Simply Liking Creativity,
isn't Living Creatively

Working adjacent to, or in proximity to, the creative field is nothing like working as a creative person or committing to a creative life.

Nowadays it is very easy to compare our lives with others. Our feeds are full of people showing off their jobs, their creative work, seemingly letting us into their lives and work. So it is suddenly natural for people to look at the lives that creatives lead and aspire to do the same as them, or better.

There is an obvious appeal to working in the creative field. Now that our work is more visible on our platforms, there are more and more people who think that they can easily do our job – without knowing or even caring how we produce the work that we do.

How many times have you heard that a child could recreate a painting by Miró or Picasso? This is how people think when they are not part of the creative process, but the reality is entirely different.

Everyone has creativity, but not everyone lives a creative life – so to compare the two is not equivalent. It is simple for someone to think they could do what we do, but they indulge in this fantasy while remaining safe on the sidelines.

To be truly creative means living and breathing it – it is second nature, because we are wired differently. We are always curious about new things and our minds are open to experience new music, art, poetry. We naturally search for new forms of expression or aesthetic. We are always adding to our skills or even working for free to be able to fulfil our internal passion to create – it's why so many of us spend weekends working but don't feel it is work, because we are creating something new.

Often those who are attracted by the appeal of a creative life, don't have what it takes to commit to it – they only want the rewards that come with the final output. But as we all know, it doesn't work that way!

Creative individuals have certain skills, and a level of emotional intelligence and sensitivity in order to create. If they didn't, they would never problem-solve in a way that is different to anyone else – they would only ever put forward solutions that are right in front of our faces. The sense of fearlessness and risk-taking that comes with putting yourself in the line of fire is something

Rejane Dal Bello

that only creatives ever do willingly.
While those who work with
creatives might think they are up to the
task, the reality is that it is a daily effort.
Simply wanting to enjoy the fruits of
creativity is not enough – you have
to be prepared to put the work in too.

"Creative individuals have certain
skills, and a level of emotional
intelligence and sensitivity
in order to create. If they didn't,
they would never problem-solve
in a way that is different to anyone
else – they would only ever put
forward solutions that are right
in front of our faces."

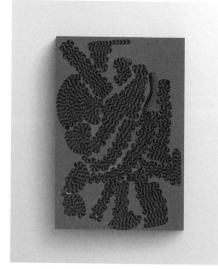

STICKER ART STREET EXHIBITION DURING COVID
This series of sticker collages on paper was created during the 2020
lockdown period and formed a free, street exhibition for residents
in the artist's neighbourhood.

Rejane Dal Bello

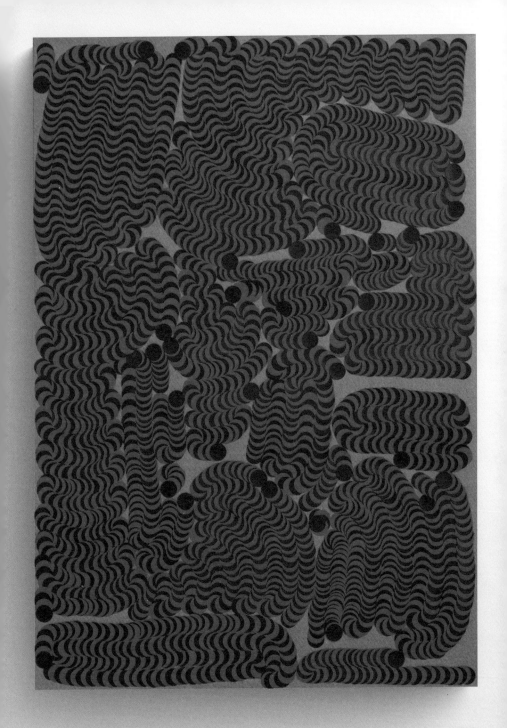

Simply Liking Creativity, isn't Living Creatively

WE CA
IDENT

N ONLY
FY

We Can Only Identify

I like the word identity... because an identity comes out of identifying what it is that makes you different and unique.

As brand designers and creators of visual identities, what I believe we do is to identify. To have an identity is to be equal. Like on an identity card: the photo on it has to match who you are for you to be identifiable and recognised by others.

So if I create a brand that does not match the core of what my client or company is, I am missing the point.

But we can only identify what is there, and what the company is. We cannot identify what is absent. So being honest when creating a brand identity is crucial.

The creative strategy highlights the core of a client's problem in words,

Rejane Dal Bello

and then it is handed over to me to do the same in images. Being honest in the strategy phase is essential, otherwise it will take us too far from the core reality that the visuals need to reach.

A brand may have its own aspirations, but a visual identity can never really express more than what it is in that moment. What we do, is to first go to the core of what the company is and from there, see where it stands moving towards the future.

"To have an identity is to be equal. Like on an identity card: the photo on it has to match who you are for you to be identifiable and recognised by others."

CITY OF DELFT

This project is a visual identity for the city of Delft in Holland. The brief was to represent the rich history of the city and its innovative character.

The logo blends traditional typography with new characters. Historical and modern silhouettes of Delft were used, which reference its local products and typography created that uses both a sans serif and a refined serif font. The use of drawn illustration represents a city that is always developing. It's an honest, heartfelt celebration.

Project developed while working at Studio Dumbar.

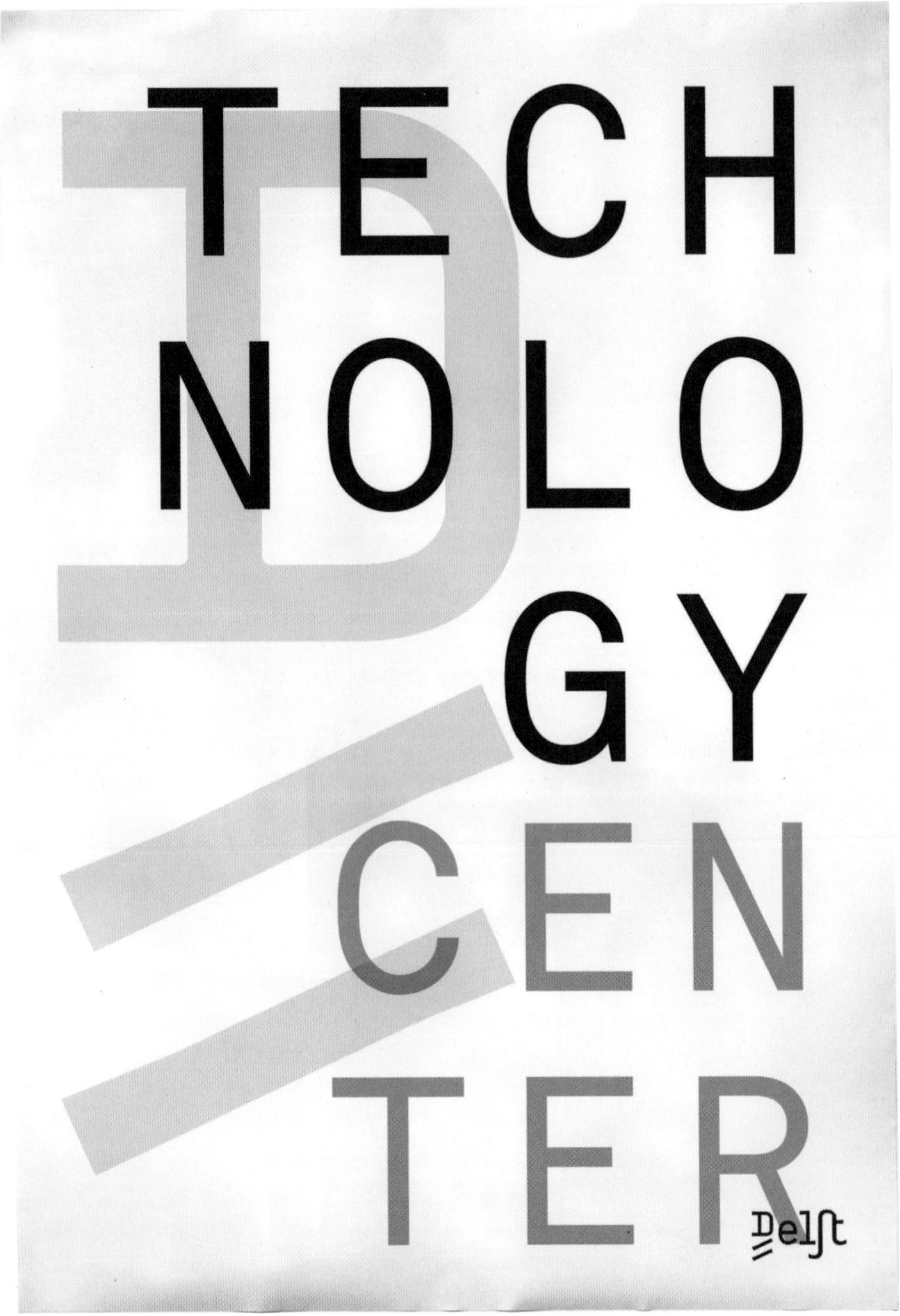

TECH
NOLO
GY
CEN
TER

Delſt

Rejane Dal Bello

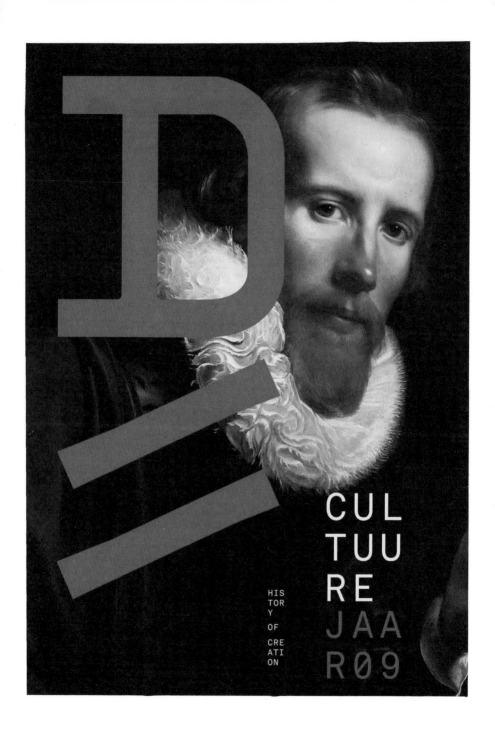

CUL
TUU
RE
JAA
R09

HIS
TOR
Y
OF
CRE
ATI
ON

We Can Only Identify

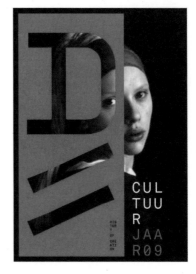

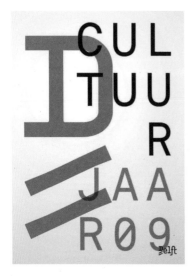
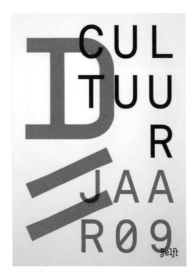

Rejane Dal Bello

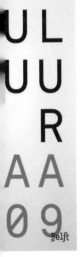
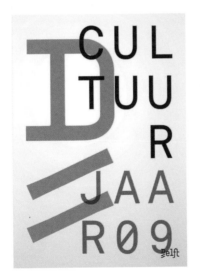

We Can Only Identify

Rejane Dal Bello

I HAT
WO
'BRAN

THE
RD
DING'

I Hate the Word 'Branding'

I was asked once in an interview, 'why don't you like the word branding?'

Trying to be diplomatic, I answered that I don't hate the word nor dislike it, when in truth, I do! It is rather, I think that it gives a problematic perception of design.

My reason is that I have been working in the field for a long time, and I have seen how 'design' has become distinct from 'branding' to the point that it has somehow turned out to be of a lesser value. Since 'branding' has become its own thing, there is a perception that designers are only dealing with forms and not thinking about what they are, or that designers need an external discipline to think for them. Both I think, are misleading.

Rejane Dal Bello

Similarly, if someone says that they develop 'visual identities', they are seen to have no value; whereas, if they say that they do 'branding' they do. For me, this is again misleading.

Design needs other disciplines to learn and grow with. Especially within the complex market we have now.

The strategic thinking and the methodology behind design has always been there, and it will continue to be. It is the core of what design means, which is to project. So I think that instead of strengthening the discipline of design, branding is weakening collective appreciation for its craft.

I think it is the same with phrases like 'design thinking'. There are now so many titles and terms to over explain what we do. There is a false hierarchy that has been created between designers, but my view has always

I Hate the Word 'Branding'

been that design does the same job no matter what the end outcome is. 'Branding' and other terms like it, are creating categories within a category, almost creating 'castes' in the process – something that I think neither elevates nor values the thinking inherent to our profession.

"Since 'branding' has become its own thing, there is a perception that designers are only dealing with forms and not thinking about what they are, or that designers need an external discipline to think for them. Both I think, are misleading."

Rejane Dal Bello

ALM

ALM is a French life
insurance company that
is non-profit – its purpose
is to support its members
through the difficult times
in their lives. The design
adapted the existing, iconic
logo into a new context,
with engaging photography
and a vibrant, versatile
colour palette. It speaks
to the life of a customer,
and ALM's job to help them
'unfold' the crucial moments
in their lives.

The first ALM rebrand took
place while working at
Studio Dumbar. The second
was carried out by Studio
Rejane Dal Bello.

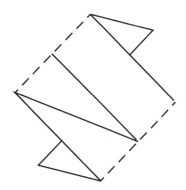

I Hate the Word 'Branding'

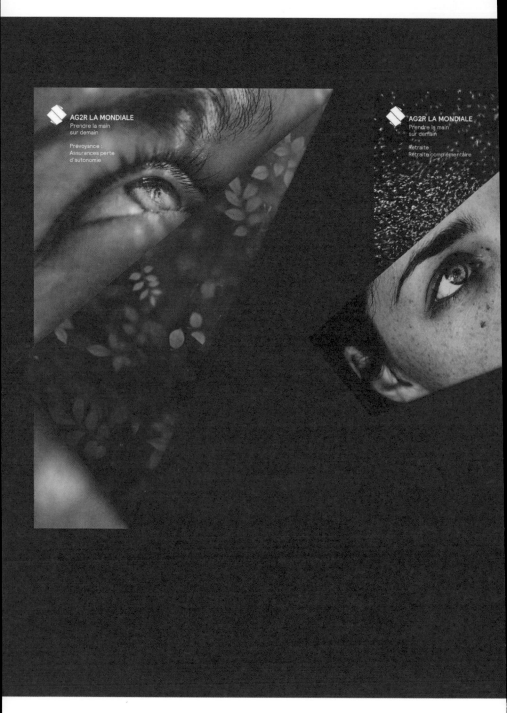

AG2R LA MONDIALE
Prendre la main
sur demain

Prévoyance :
Assurances perte
d'autonomie

AG2R LA MONDIALE
Prendre la main
sur demain

Retraite :
Retraite complémentaire

Rejane Dal Bello

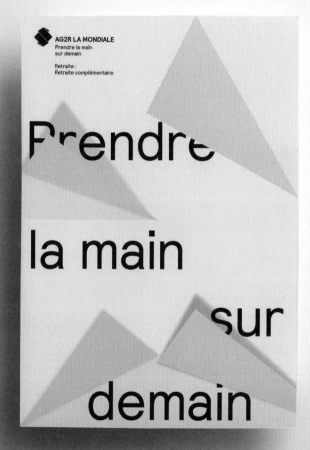

ÊTRE UNIQUE

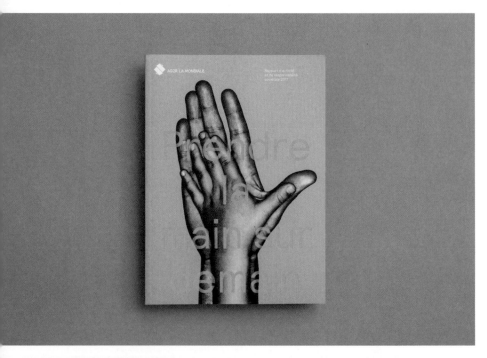

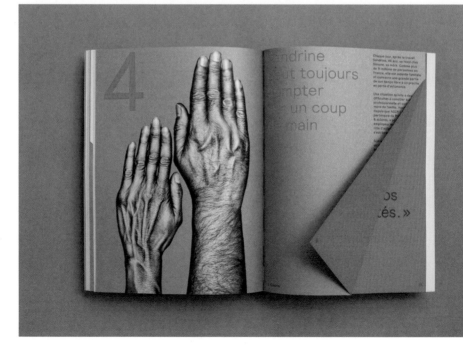

Rejane Dal Bello

BEAU
HONI

TY IS
ESTY

Beauty is Honesty

I believe beauty is really important to design, but I think we tend to diminish the value of its role. The truth is, beauty requires honest work.

Truly iconic work is both honest and beautiful, because honesty is beauty.
We respond to and understand images emotionally, not intellectually. So I believe that an image or design piece can only be loved when it has been born out of a truly honest approach that can be felt and seen. Beauty alone, with no content or strong concept, has no meaning.
Beauty is important; therefore design is important – because it is one of the professions that requires you have to have the intelligence of a problem solver and the special sensitivity of an artist.

Rejane Dal Bello

artistiek leider Candida Thompson

Amsterdam Sinfonietta

Kristine Blaumane
Christophe Coin
Alexander Rudin
cello

mahlers
laatste
adem

maandag 20 oktober 20.30 uur
Muziekgebouw aan 't IJ

reserveren 020 788 20 00
www.sinfonietta.nl

randstad
hoofdsponsor

Beauty is Honesty

The Amsterdam Symphony has an enviable international reputation and a broad repertoire, performing everything from baroque to contemporary music.

The posters designed for the Symphony were driven by a bold logotype and typographic palette. This helped showcase the dramatically different artists and performances, while retaining a strong, instantly recognisable identity.

Project developed while working at Studio Dumbar.

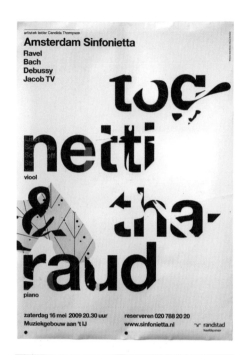

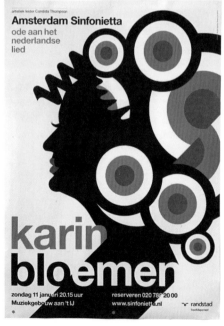

Rejane Dal Bello

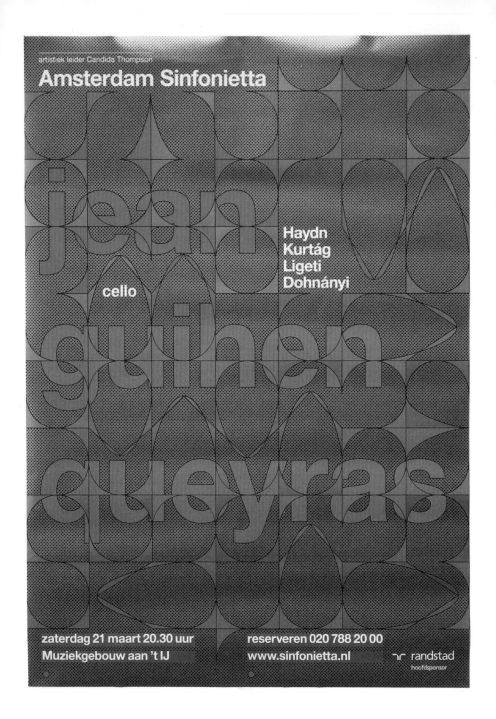

artistiek leider Candida Thompson

Amsterdam Sinfonietta

jean

cello

Haydn
Kurtág
Ligeti
Dohnányi

guihen

queyras

zaterdag 21 maart 20.30 uur
Muziekgebouw aan 't IJ

reserveren 020 788 20 00
www.sinfonietta.nl

randstad
hoofdsponsor

Rejane Dal Bello

Amsterdam Sinfonietta

artistiek leider Candida Thompson

isabelle van
viool
keuler &
ronald
brautigam
piano

zaterdag 15 maart 20.30 uur   reserveren 020 788 20 00
Muziekgebouw aan 't IJ   www.sinfonietta.nl

⅂ᴦ randstad
hoofdsponsor

Rejane Dal Bello

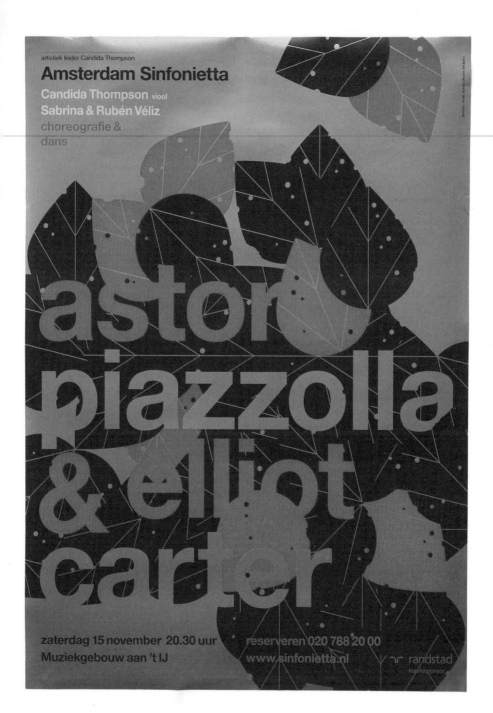

Beauty is Honesty

OUR BURDEN IS A LOSS

IS ALSO OUR STRENGTH

Our Burden is Also our Strength

As professional designers, we constantly strive to be unique. We are often found asking ourselves, what is it that only I am good at? What special skills or value do I have to offer?

I think these are all fair questions to ask ourselves from time to time, but it is also a double-edged sword.
What is special about us, and the things that are considered our strengths, also often end up being a burden that weighs us down. Because who we are ends up being both the root of our pride and the source of others' criticism. This can make it hard to keep going and keep your head held high at the same time.
We live in a society that wants everyone to be uniform, so naturally we want to be part of the group and

feel accepted. If you have a strong point of view, voicing it can sometimes be quite lonely.

I always felt like a foreigner among others in my own life, so this feeling is something I have been living with for a long time. From childhood, I have always had to prove that my approach is worth it, both to myself and to others. Feeling like an outsider actually gave me knowledge of who I am, which has kept me strong in the face of what other people have thought I maybe should have been or become, and gave me a strong will (sometimes too strong) to keep doing and believing in what I do.

I now know that I will not please everyone, but I also know that people exist who sincerely see me for my true values and who I am. That matters, and most of the time, makes this burden a little easier to carry.

Ag2r La Mondiale (ALM) is
a key sponsor of La Transat,
a prestigious international
yacht race. But it's a huge
sponsorship area for many
finance companies, so it's
hard for brands not to get
lost in the crowd.

This identity ignores every
financial branding cliché,
and takes inspiration from
the world of yacht racing.
The visual alphabet of sailing
flags was used to create a
design system that positioned
ALM as a bold, expressive
and decisive leader.

Project developed while
working at Studio Dumbar.

Rejane Dal Bello

Our Burden is Also our Strength

JCDecaux

AG2R LA MONDIALE

T R A
N S A
T 2 0
A N S

CONCARNEAU – SAINT-BARTH
DÉPART 21 AVRIL 2012

LA TRANSAT
AG2R LA MONDIALE

Our Burden is Also our Strength

Rejane Dal Bello

EU EO COSMOS

CESC COSMOS

This poster wrapped a monthly brochure, and was designed to promote special courses about space. The design places the cosmos within an image which becomes 3D when it's moved and folded by a reader – referencing the multi-dimensional nature of the cosmos.

Rejane Dal Bello

DESIGN
HIDDEN
THE W

RS ARE
BEHIND
WORK

Designers are Hidden Behind the Work

Our work is an extension of us, but it is not 'us' per se. We are hidden behind the work, and I frequently question what this means. Is it of importance whether a piece of work is done by a woman or a man? When we find out it is a woman's work, why do we tend to devalue it in comparison to a man's?

In graphic design at least, I don't see why gender distinctions continue to be so important. The work should speak for itself, and should not be judged according to the gender of the designer who made it.

In theory at least, design is a perfect model of a profession that should embrace diversity at all levels. It thrives on the fact that we need to

Rejane Dal Bello

see things from different perspectives, and to see new things means we need people who are different, not all the same. We are thirsty for new approaches and new ideas – staying in our bubble we cannot achieve that.

One of the most masculine projects I have worked on to date is a racing sponsorship for a massive male-focused brand. If I didn't tell you I was behind it, you would never know it had been done by a woman – there is nothing remotely feminine or delicate about it. And that's how I believe it should be. As long as a designer has done their job well, it should not matter who they are, what their age, gender, race or anything else is. The outcome should be the sole focus of anyone's attention.

The only time that I feel that I personally need to know who is behind the work is when a design is done disrespectfully. A few years ago, the official kit for Colombia's female cycling team was re-designed, with only their brand sponsors displayed at the top and the rest of the kit in flesh tones, to create the illusion that they were otherwise naked. It was an obvious PR stunt to attract more TV ratings and literally keep eyes on the team, because competitive women's cycling is a relatively new concept. It is in such situations that I want to know: who the hell is the designer that did this to them?

Design is supposed to enhance, not to diminish a product or person. In this case, serious professionals who have dedicated their life to a sport were made to appear less than they really are, on the biggest day of their careers, simply because of a thoughtless piece of design.

Colombia's female cycling team kit. Designer unknown.

When used in this way, design can destroy the very thing that it is meant to elevate. It is not acceptable to bring the profession into disrepute because your design calls attention to something for the wrong reasons, or because you wanted to be provocative for its own sake. As designers, we always have a choice – and we have a responsibility to use our craft carefully and well.

ALM TOUR DE FRANCE

How do you create an identity that works when it's always moving? This project for the Ag2r La Mondiale (ALM) Tour De France team meant branding objects that most people see flying past on their screens.

The strength of this identity lies in the iconic logo, the expressive typography and the bold use of colour. Visual clichés associated with the financial sector were purposely avoided and instead the decision was made to reference the dot pattern of the Tour jerseys as a tribute to the event.

The first ALM rebrand took place while working at Studio Dumbar. The second was carried out by Studio Rejane Dal Bello.

Rejane Dal Bello

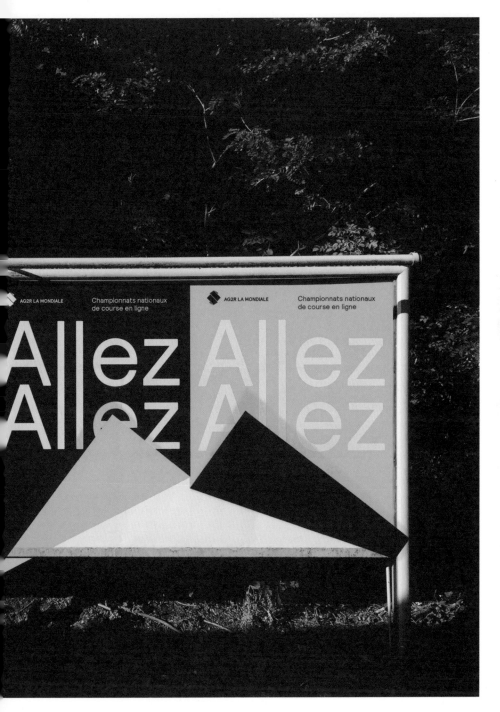

Designers are Hidden Behind the Work

YOU CAN LOOK LOOK

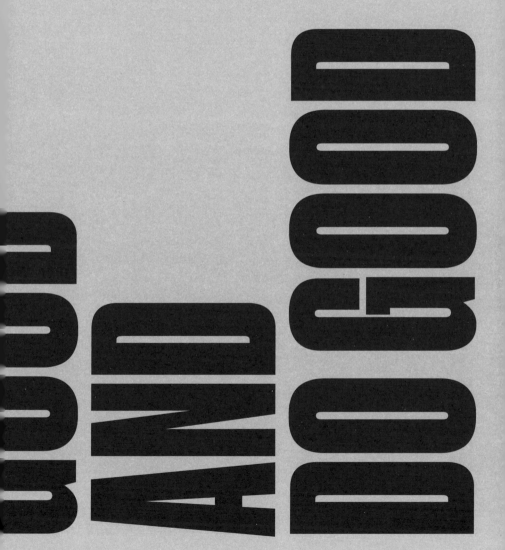

You Can Look Good and Do Good

Last year I developed a visual identity that I am really proud of. It started really unusually: I joined as a volunteer for a non-profit organisation called The Smile Brigade. Their mission is to bring joy, food, and run activities for the elderly, homeless or less fortunate.

I was put into a group of volunteers that spend their afternoons going to care homes, giving company to the elderly and putting on dancing and karaoke afternoons. Many of the care home residents had dementia and it was quite a lonely place for them. But through her volunteers, the young girl that founded The Smile Brigade brought joy to them. It was quite special and I got to be involved a lot for a period of time, especially as my studio was not super busy at that time.

While I was there, I learned more about how she needed to grow her business in order to be taken more seriously. Her goal was to be able to get a bigger grant from the government so she could help more people.

Moments like these are when we designers can help, and where we probably offer the most help to other companies and institutions: in helping them to be more solid, and be taken more seriously through their image in the first instance.

The Smile Brigade already had a brand identity, which at that point was two hands facing each other and almost touching. It was quite a melancholy image, despite their positive brand name and the accompanying tagline, 'bringing smiles'.

In other words, the image of her company was not really translating the value she brought, which is literally a feeling of joy to vulnerable people through TSB volunteers.

Having seen for myself how her brand did not match her needs, I decided to develop an identity anyway and see what she thought afterwards. Afterwards, I told her I had developed a brand identity for her, which I thought would help her company to take its next step.

She loved it when I showed her, and even started to use it in some of her business proposals.

But as with anyone that is used to an old way of doing things, there was a fear of change that sat beneath her initial response. After thinking about it, she told me that a non-profit could not look good, otherwise she will look too expensive. We had an interesting conversation, in which I tried to persuade her that it is not about looking bad or good; it is about looking professional. She needed to communicate what her current brand identity was lacking, so people would notice The Smile Brigade and associate the amazing work she was doing with the image she was presenting to the world.

Like any small business, though she started the company, she is not the company. Neither is she her brand: she is the source of the idea that it is based on, but it is an extension of her – and the two need to be clear and separate.

Then came the day a government official went to inspect the work she was doing, to assess her for the possibility of funding a community soup kitchen. After they arrived, they praised how professional her brand looked, and told her that it made them more certain that she was for real and not a fake.

She immediately texted me to relay their comments, and how she finally understood the power of a good brand identity to make her stand out.

In this case, a brand is not only a logo. It is a promise. It tells others that your service is good, your image is strong, and you are able to live up to expectations. There are plenty of amazing identities out there which don't line up with the companies they represent. They are not brands, simply companies that have a nice logo.

The symbol carries a lot for a company. It is the symbol that binds together the idea and the ideology of a place, and reminds employees what they work for and why they are working for it. It is a visual umbrella that brings everyone together underneath it.

Now every Tuesday, since receiving funds to open their community kitchen,

Rejane Dal Bello

The Smile Brigade take a group picture – with the team and every volunteer who helped that day, gathered around their company banner. They can proudly stand beside The Smile Brigade logo, as the symbol of something they all believe in and that they are happy to be a part of.

"A brand is not only a logo. It is a promise. It tells others that your service is good, your image is strong, and you are able to live up to expectations."

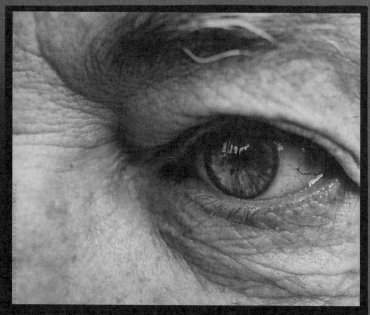

CHECK US OUT AT
WWW.THESMILEBRIGADE.ORG
WWW.GOFUNDME.COM/THESMILEBRIGADE

THE
SMILE
BRIGADE

Rejane Dal Bello

THE SMILE BRIGADE
This non-profit voluntary organisation offers vulnerable people
a range of help and services - everything from freshly cooked meals
to haircuts.

The visual identity work graphically represents the idea of people
working together. It's moving, simple and welcoming.

You Can Look Good and Do Good

CHECK US OUT AT
WWW.THESMILEBRIGADE.ORG
WWW.GOFUNDME.COM/THESMILEBRIGADE

THE ●　●
SMILE
BRIGADE

Rejane Dal Bello

CHECK US OUT AT
WWW.THESMILEBRIGADE.ORG
WWW.GOFUNDME.COM/THESMILEBRIGADE

THE SMILE BRIGADE

You Can Look Good and Do Good

THE SMILE BRIGADE

Rejane Dal Bello

You Can Look Good and Do Good

Rejane Dal Bello

DESIGN I
BECA
YOU M

ATTERS,
USE
ATTER

CITIZEN FIRST,
DESIGNER SECOND

Written by Rejane Dal Bello

Revised by Jayshree
Viswanathan

ISBN
978-1-8381865-0-0

DESIGN
Céline Leterme
Jon Dowling

PHOTOGRAPHY
Ag2r La Mondiale: Pg 310-311,
312-113
Mel Duarte: Pg 1, 4, 7, 10-11,
28-29, 90-91, 92-93, 94,
96, 124-125, 133, 134-135,
154-155, 156, 182-183,
184-185, 276-277
Aad Hoogendoorn: Pg 242
Anna Huix: Pg 8-9, 112-113,
114-115, 116-117
Danny Kreeft: Pg 197, 198-199
Otis LA: Pg 186-187
Xenia Naselos: Pg 180-181
Antje Peters: Pg 123, 126-127
Gerrit Schreurs: Pg 46-47,
188-189, 190-191
Edouard Stéru: Pg 292-293,
294-295, 296-297, 298-299
Pim Top: Pg 58-59, 61, 62-63
Fernando Vergara/
Shutterstock: Pg 309

Copyright on all project
imagery is held by Rejane
Dal Bello.

TYPEFACES
Druk Condensed Super
Suisse Int'l
Suisse Int'l Mono

REJANE DAL BELLO
→ rejanedalbello.com

COUNTER-PRINT
→ counter-print.co.uk

© 2020 Counter-Print

First published in the
United Kingdom in 2020
by Counter-Print.

British Library
cataloguing-in-publication
data: A catalogue of this
book can be found in the
British Library.